Becoming a Powerhouse Librarian

Medical Library Association Books

The Medical Library Association (MLA) features books that showcase the expertise of health sciences librarians for other librarians and professionals.

MLA Books are excellent resources for librarians in hospitals, medical research practice, and other settings. These volumes will provide health care professionals and patients with accurate information that can improve outcomes and save lives.

Each book in the series has been overseen editorially since conception by the Medical Library Association Books Panel, composed of MLA members with expertise spanning the breadth of health sciences librarianship.

Medical Library Association Books Panel

Kristen L. Young, AHIP, chair
Dorothy Ogdon, AHIP, chair designate
Michel C. Atlas
Carolann Lee Curry
Kelsey Leonard, AHIP
Karen McElfresh, AHIP
Dorothy C. Ogdon, AHIP
JoLinda L. Thompson, AHIP
Heidi Heilemann, AHIP, board liaison

About the Medical Library Association

Founded in 1898, MLA is a 501(c)(3) nonprofit, educational organization of 3,500 individual and institutional members in the health sciences information field that provides lifelong educational opportunities, supports a knowledgebase of health information research, and works with a global network of partners to promote the importance of quality information for improved health to the health care community and the public.

Books in the Series:

Becoming a Powerhouse Librarian

How to Get Things Done Right the First Time

Jamie M. Gray

ROWMAN & LITTLEFIELD
Lanham • Boulder • New York • London

Published by Rowman & Littlefield
A wholly owned subsidiary of The Rowman & Littlefield Publishing Group, Inc.
4501 Forbes Boulevard, Suite 200, Lanham, Maryland 20706
www.rowman.com

Unit A, Whitacre Mews, 26-34 Stannary Street, London SE11 4AB

British Library Cataloguing in Publication Information Available

Library of Congress Cataloging-in-Publication Data Available

ISBN 9781442278684 (hardback : alk. paper) | ISBN 9781442278691 (pbk. : alk. paper) | ISBN 9781442278707 (electronic)

∞™ The paper used in this publication meets the minimum requirements of American National Standard for Information Sciences—Permanence of Paper for Printed Library Materials, ANSI/NISO Z39.48-1992.

Printed in the United States of America

Contents

Acknowledgments

I wanted to take a moment to acknowledge all of the people who helped me through this creative process to bring an actual book to fruition. It was a long process, which I could not have undertaken without the expertise and contributions of so many.

First, I'd like to offer a most sincere thanks to the librarians willing to share their true powerhouse experiences. Your concrete, approachable examples brought so much realness to the concepts the book discusses. You are examples of true powerhouse librarians not only for what you have been able to accomplish but also for the kindness and generosity of spirit you so willingly share with colleagues such as myself.

Second, this book would not have been possible without the colleagues and individuals who so graciously supported me as I worked to develop my voice and craft the message I wanted to share. I want to acknowledge Josh for his superior editorial skills and willingness to build me a template so I could just focus on the writing. And I want to thank Jeannie, Dick, Nicole, and David for providing feedback on various drafts; your insights and questions helped me explore new pathways and craft content I'm truly proud of. And finally I thank Charles, for his flexibility and willingness to help me stay on track, despite life's little detours.

Third, I would not have had the confidence to pursue such an undertaking without the solid and supportive mentors and colleagues, both new and old, with whom I've had the privilege of working and of whom there are too many to list here. Your guidance, humor, creativity, and encouragement have been vital to this creative process and my career at large. I have learned so much about the art of "getting things done" from all of you. Thank you for being my teachers, colleagues, and friends.

And finally last, but certainly not least, I thank my loving family, in particular, my husband Matt, the best partner I ever could have hoped for. Without all of you, my efforts would be for naught. You are the motivation and inspiration that keeps me going every day. Thank you for your endless supply of love, encouragement, and support. You are my world.

Introduction

Becoming a powerhouse librarian is not for the faint of heart. The process requires creativity, perseverance, the ability to laugh at one's self, and the ability to gain the trust of those around you. I wrote this book because I believe everyone has the potential to improve satisfaction at work (and in life) by contributing in a meaningful way. Improving your effectiveness is something we are all capable of—regardless of the world around us.

The contents of *Becoming a Powerhouse Librarian: How to Get Things Done Right the First Time* were shaped by an accumulation of experiences and observations gleaned throughout my career. I am truly humbled to be able to share these thoughts and insights with you.

Becoming a Powerhouse Librarian identifies specific behaviors and habits that you can cultivate to get things done in your organization. Regardless of job title, rank, or library type, we all desire to be effective and make a difference for our users. Inside you'll find stories and insights from real professionals in the field, as well as templates and tips you can utilize in your own practice. Each chapter focuses on a different skill, mind-set, or behavior needed to successfully accomplish your professional (and personal) to-do list.

If you see yourself as any of the following, then this book is intended for you:

- A lifelong learner
- Someone who knows they might fail but is willing to go after his or her desires anyway

- A cheerleader to those around them
- Someone who believes it's never too late to try
- Someone who has a desire to be any of the above and more

Becoming a Powerhouse Librarian is organized into overarching themes readers need to be aware of when striving to get things done. The following is a brief overview of the specific topics each chapter covers.

- Chapter 1 focuses on cultivating an attitude of inquiry and the importance of lifelong learning. Charting a course to keeping current is essential to staying nimble in today's fast-paced world.
- Chapter 2 discusses the need to embrace change and take calculated risks on a daily basis. Readers are encouraged to have an open mind to what the end results will be. Unexpected outcomes or "failures" can be reflected on through "lessons learned" analysis to inform future decision making or planning.
- Chapter 3 discusses ways readers can tap into their creative side. Ways to both enhance the process and envision new and expanded roles will be included.
- Chapter 4 challenges readers to evaluate how they network, both inside and outside the library.
- Chapter 5 addresses identifying and engaging with project stakeholders. Content includes ideas for further developing relationships and the importance of communication.
- Chapter 6 discusses the need for finding balance both at work and personally. This topic is an essential skill that needs to be continually honed for long-term productivity.
- Chapter 7 focuses on working within a team environment. In addition to discussing building well-functioning teams, this chapter will encourage readers to develop a personal SWOT analysis.
- Chapter 8 takes the discussion from chapter 7 one step further to address the issue of leadership. The topics of followership, styles, building core leadership qualities, and leading while not in a position of authority are discussed.
- Chapter 9 challenges readers to reenvision their jobs in terms of building skill sets rather than job titles. As the library environment continues to change, so will the roles we find ourselves in. By shift-

ing our attention to developing a personal, growing skill toolkit rather than the narrow definition of a job title, we will better be able to meet the demands of the future.

- Chapter 10 concludes by discussing the power of attitude. Topics covered include burnout, dealing with setbacks, and cultivating mindfulness and resiliency.

Whether you're just beginning your career as a librarian or are a seasoned professional, I hope you'll find *Becoming a Powerhouse Librarian: How to Get Things Done Right the First Time* has something for everyone and will help improve both your efficiency and your happiness in work and in life.

1

Taking the Road Less Traveled

Lifelong Learning and Getting out of Your Comfort Zone

How This Might Look in Practice:

- Attainment of different levels of Academy of Health Information Professionals (AHIP) certification
- Implementation of communities of practice (e.g., instruction, user experience)
- Getting a graduate certificate in scholarly communication, copyright, and so forth

The capacity to learn is one of the greatest hallmarks of humanity. No other earthly species has the ability to gather data, think critically, or generate shareable knowledge to the extent that we do. Go team humanity! We directly influence our sphere of knowledge by the choices we make every day. And let's be honest, life nowadays is all about the choices. Whom we choose to interact with, what we consume through the media, and what we read on our tablets all have a hand in developing our mental lens for viewing the world. There is a never-ending supply of information and knowledge to acquire. We, both society and libraries, have effectively moved from the industrial age through the information age to an age focused on translation. Today we are squarely in the transformation age with no end in sight. Transformation is directly impacted by our ability to learn. And in libraries the need to learn is always ongoing.

The *Oxford English Dictionary* defines learning as "the acquisition of knowledge or skills through experience, study, or by being taught." This

Important Tip

In addition to both acquiring and applying knowledge, it is essential to actually build in time for repetition. The phrase "practice makes perfect" didn't come into fashion for nothing.

description makes room to capture everyday experiences as an opportunity to learn. The ability to acquire knowledge (or brain candy as most librarians know it) is the first important step in the learning process. We need to be able to retain said nuggets in order to utilize them later. At a most basic level our ability to learn (and hopefully connect learning) is what keeps us safe. Although we usually think of this type of functioning as "common sense," that ability is rooted in our capacity to learn. Collecting diverse nuggets allows us to build a broad foundational understanding from which to form judgments and make decisions, big and small (Herrmann et al. 2007). It is the reservoir from which we can mix and match our learning nuggets to address the situation before us. However, gathering that sweet, sweet knowledge is only step one. True powerhouse librarians know that learning is a multipart process.

To be effective today librarians must not only acquire the right knowledge but also apply that learning. Knowledge without application is like having a match but refusing to spark it. The possibilities for light, warmth, creation, or destruction are all there, but that potential is dormant until someone chooses to strike the match to life. Likewise, knowledge can't fully be realized until it is put into action. The application process is what actually develops our skills, creates a library service, or brings a new information product to market. If knowledge is the dough, then the application is the oven. You don't get something edible until both are combined.

Now that the basics are out of the way, we can get to the truly important part. You might be wondering why we are spending the first chapter of this book talking about learning. We are librarians after all, and educating is a big part of what we do. Committing to become a lifelong learner is a requirement of the profession. Okay, you caught me. Technically it's not, but it really should be. True powerhouse librarians know that lifelong learning is vital to ensuring our profession remains responsive and agile. Why? Everything changes, nothing is static forever. What it meant to be a librarian fifty years ago is certainly not the same today. Curriculums for MLS and MLIS programs shift dramatically. We now have an "I" in our credentials! What was taught to a graduate student in 2000 is likely not the same focus as what students are learning today. Developing a passion for lifelong learning early in your career is the best way to safeguard both your and the profession's longevity. By recognizing and embracing the reality of our perpetual "studenthood" from the onset, you will be better positioned to take on the rapid changes happening to libraries.

FLAVORS OF LEARNING

If you have participated in any kind of structured learning in the recent past, you are likely aware of and influenced by different styles of learning. Since the early 1980s Howard Gardner's theory of multiple intelligences has greatly impacted the way instructors have approached their teaching. His original theory asserts that people can display their intelligence in one or more of the following ways: musical, visual, verbal, logical, kinesthetic, interpersonal, and intrapersonal. Learners are typically a blended combination of these abilities (Gardner and Hatch 1989). Modern classroom learning activities are designed to appeal to a combination of these various styles. Pedagogical methods such as small-group discussions, lecture, video, hands-on practice, and journaling are all stock standard practices in education today. In fact, you've probably employed a number of these modalities in your own learning or library teaching.

In addition to the idea of presenting materials in a variety of formats that lend themselves to a wider audience of learners, changes in the actual mode of teaching are influencing the learning landscape as well. Continual advances in technology are spurring the growth of online learning. Hybridized and completely digital learning experiences are rapidly gaining in popularity. Entire universities and degree programs are going virtual in an attempt to provide flexibility to today's learner. In 2014, *Forbes* ran an article projecting online learning to reach $107 billion during 2015 (McCue, 2014).We currently have a veritable smorgasbord of choices to get learning customized "your way." So where does this leave you in determining your lifelong learning path?

Determining what works for you on the lifelong learning front is not too different then from determining your previous academic road. By this point in your librarian learning lifecycle you should have a pretty clear idea about how you learn best. If you're a learning by doing kind of person, that is unlikely to change. However, there may be new considerations you need to take into account that may influence your educational options such as release time, course length, employer firewalls, additional coursework, and so on. Personal and professional circumstances cannot be overlooked when pondering new learning opportunities.

THE STRATEGY OF DEVELOPMENT

It's not enough to simply commit to the idea of lifelong learning. True powerhouse librarians know they need a learning plan of action. With so many competing interests and priorities, finding time to actually participate in learning opportunities can be challenging. Unless you or library administration has spent money on attendance or coursework when something urgent rises to the top of the pile, for many of us, continuing education is the easiest thing to let go of. It's not that we don't value the opportunity to grow; many, many librarians participate in continuing education. The problem comes down to time. Do I plan for the future or take care of the present? Or more realistically, do I work on learning how to develop guidelines of care or complete the patient-care search for Dr. Lee's early morning appointment tomorrow? The here and now creates a sense of urgency that the future rarely musters (there are exceptions of course). It's the old battle many of us are familiar with between concrete and abstraction.

Creating a strategy for personal development is one way to combat this bias. How? We do this by reframing long-term future goals into short-term executable objectives. The problem with the future is that it's nebulous. Goals change. Pathways are unclear. Something that was supposed to happen doesn't. This unpredictability in our libraries can distract us into procrastination. And procrastinating is the nemesis to getting things done. Planning how we will stay on course for continuing education, professional development, lifelong learning, or whatever you want to call it creates accountability. When we feel accountable we are more likely to see things through. Developing a plan or strategy moves that commitment from the future to the present. Our intent is abstract, but a plan is concrete.

To build an effective development strategy you must know yourself (this will be a running theme throughout this book). This is not to say that you have to know exactly who you are and what you want to be when you grow up. Heck, I'm still figuring that out eleven plus years into the profession! But knowing yourself well enough to know general goals, what motivates you, what doesn't, your preferences, abilities, likes, and dislikes will be important to developing a successful and doable plan. If it doesn't resonate, then you won't do it. To help you get started on developing your personalized plan, ask yourself the following:

- What is my ultimate goal?
- What might be influencing that goal (internally and externally)?
- What do I need to make that happen (e.g., degree)?
- What do I currently know and what do I need to learn?
- What is the time commitment now and in the future?
- What is my timeline?
- What other things will I need to balance this with?
- What are my learning options?
- How do I learn best?
- Am I passionate about what I'm pursuing?

Obviously there are other questions you might wish to consider adding on topics such as funding, life situations, organizational goals, and so forth, that can help inform your strategy. Some of this information may end up being a part of your strategy, but the goal of the above activity is to help you assess the influences that may pose barriers in the future. Now that you have an idea of your influences, it's time to jump into what learning options are potentially at your disposal.

Important Tip

Make sure to allow for some flexibility in your strategy. The goal of getting your plan out on paper is to make it real, not binding. Make adjustments as needed.

Talking about lifelong learning is like talking about ice cream flavors at Baskin Robbins. There are generally enough options to satisfy everyone, regardless of whether you're a chocolate, vanilla, or specialty flavor fan. In today's day and age we have access to learning in an unprecedented way. We have direct control over what and how we learn. We can customize degree programs, content format, credit options, synchronicity, and more. Where education used to be all about the institution, today it is about the individual. So how do you decide what is right for you?

This is where knowing yourself and your end goal comes into play in a serious way. Selecting your method for learning will likely be influenced by a variety of personal and professional factors. For instance,

- Are you someone who needs a lot of personal interaction with an instructor and other students?
- Do you need flexibility for when and where you learn?
- Are you brushing up old library skills or trying to acquire new ones?
- Why are you pursuing these learning opportunities? Accreditation? Career advancement?
- Are you looking for theoretical or practical training?

Each answer can help puzzle together your learning path. Below are the most frequently thought of learning options one might pursue. If you are in the earlier stages of your library career, it's likely that you will utilize all of these types of learning at some point (if you haven't already).

To start, let's talk about the "traditional" education route. Now, if you are a degreed librarian you should already have a pretty good idea of what this type of learning entails. I'm defining "traditional" as the standard collegiate experience. Traditional learning starts with the identification of a program of interest (degree or certificate) and the standard rigmarole of qualifying and applying to the program. The type of program you are enrolling in, if you're pursuing the program full or part time, the institution's policies regarding transfer or "real world" credit, the academic calendar the institution adheres to, course offerings, course prerequisites, and completion requirements will all be factors that influence the length of time until you score that shiny new degree (or certificate). However, this is not the only time factor to consider. Course hours (in person or online) also need to be factored into the equation. Finding time to attend "lectures," review required materials, complete coursework, and study all eat up time out of your twenty-four-hour day. Answering the time question is critical to successfully pursuing this course. Why? Time (and of course money but more on that later) will influence every facet of your learning experience from course load to degree completion.

Pursuing a "traditional" education is a large and laborious undertaking but comes with a very tangible benefit: a degree. Depending on your career goals, employer requirements, or just personal interests, this might be the best option to advance personally, professionally, spiritually, or what have you. Although the current degree for librarianship is considered terminal, many librarians choose to pursue more formal education to help them on the job. For some, additional education can translate into subject expertise or leadership advancement or can expand their employment options outside of the library setting. Knowing what your end goals are can help you decide if the formal route is right for you.

If your learning needs are more acute than chronic, finding less formal avenues of learning may be more appealing. Some examples of more informal learning opportunities include

- Mentoring
- Online MOOCs (massive open online courses)
- Continuing education via professional organizations
- Reviewing the literature
- Shadowing
- Learning by doing (e.g., pilot projects)
- Workshops
- Institutes

Now to be fair, the options listed above are fluid in their informalness. MOOCs (massive open online courses) and continuing education (CE) can certainly be pursued in an attempt to achieve some higher level. For example, the Medical Library Association has a designated CE curriculum for those who want to pursue certain specializations such as consumer health or disaster preparedness. What sets that apart from more "traditional" education can be found in the cost, time, accreditation, and accountability factor. Still not sure what I mean? The pursuit of a CE specialization (or even just CE in general) is entirely up to me. How fast I go, courses I take, or whether I even finish all rest on my motivation. There are no formal systems in place, such as an advisor or peer cohort, to guide me along my learning journey. Where traditional learning is like a plated dinner, informal forms offer up a Brazilian-style steakhouse experience. You consume as much or as little as you like at your own pace.

Where the strength of traditional education lies in the granting of a degree, the flexibility and adaptability that informal learning opportunities supply cannot be overlooked. They afford us the chance to quickly tune up as new challenges surface. These experiences also allow us to sample new areas of learning we may not know we'd ever need. See the case example below for how this might play out "real world" style.

> I seek out professional development and learning opportunities in two areas: continuing education classes that are in alignment with both my current position and "larger view" opportunities that speak to my longer-term goals or to areas in which I want to grow in order to be a better professional overall. For example, when I took on my current position, I became much more of a project manager than I have been in the past. I took a project management class that provided good tools and concepts so that I could grow in that particular area of my job. In terms of my longer-term career, however, I tend to seek out workshops and institutes that will support me as I continue to grow and advance. One example of this would be the Leadership Institute I attended a couple years ago. It was a weeklong intensive experience, at the end of which I was able to clearly articulate my goals for growth over the next several years. (GK)

As continuous change becomes more a staple of the library landscape, dabbling or even immersing ourselves in new content will become a standard part of the job, regardless of specialty. Continuing education activities are a great way to sample content and determine if more learning is required. Think of it as the try-it-before-you-buy-it model of learning. And this is a great segue into our next topic—the dreaded funding discussion.

FUNDING AND YOU

One of the great things about how easy education is to access today is that there is a learning opportunity for every budget. Regardless of your

Important Tip

The Internet truly does offer a wide variety of freely available learning opportunities. Depending on what you're looking for, investigating standards such as YouTube, TED, professional organizations, and government websites are a solid bet in identifying quality, timely content. Just make sure to apply the same super-sleuth principles you always do in evaluating the Web for authority, authenticity, and awesomeness.

ability to fork over your hard-earned cash, something is available to feed your learning hunger pains, whether it is a class, workshop, webinar, presentation, or just the Internet. Free versus fee no longer has to be an obstacle. Although let's be honest, sometimes it still is, especially depending on what you're trying to achieve (e.g., a second masters, MLA AHIP accreditation, certification, etc.). For this section we're going to address resources and strategies for sussing out money when needed. True powerhouse librarians know there are a variety of ways to get your hands on funding if needed; it takes a bit more effort but produces a wealth of reward in the end.

For many, if personal funds aren't being used, the usual suspect for learning support is your employer. Depending on what type of library you work in (e.g., public versus academic) your level of training support can vary. Reasons that may influence allocations could include classification and rank, budget, promotion and tenure status and requirements, number of employees, type of learning opportunity, relationship to your current position, and so on. Knowing where your employer stands on professional development is one of the first things you should find out—even as early as the interview.

If you don't have a specific allocation assigned to you within the library's budget, take heart. There may be other avenues to find money for learning within your organization if you know where to look. One good source of funding to investigate is your benefits package. Many employers, particularly those with an academic focus, provide some type of support for learning development (particularly if it is job related). Possible options could include tuition waiver or remission for you and dependents, free classes taught through organizational development, and so forth. In addition, many employers often have special entities you may be able to solicit for funds. For example, there may be training pots of money you could apply for through groups such as organizational development, center for teaching and learning, or the faculty and staff development office.

Exploring funding options outside of your library is also a smart bet. Many professional organizations offer awards and scholarships. The one caveat is that typically you must be a member. These opportunities can cover activities ranging from taking classes to attendance at the annual meeting. Each organization's rules and applications will vary, but oftentimes a statement of need, the funding's impact on you and your organization, and so forth, are part of the evaluation process. In addition

Table 1.1.   Lifelong-Learning Activity Assessment
Define your Learning Objective (aka what you want to learn):

Program Type	Pros	Cons	Current Personal Situation	Overall Score
In person				
Online				
Credit				
Noncredit				
MOOC				
Continuing ed				
Lecture				
Hands on				
Simulation				

To Score: Add +1 point for each pro; −1 for each con; +0.5 of a point for each positive life situation (assets); −0.5 of a point for each negative life situation (barriers).

Examples:

Asset = PTO for training, supportive partner

Barrier = Time, needing to travel

to these organizations, other entities, such as the National Network of Libraries of Medicine's (NN/LM) regional medical libraries and similar groups, sometimes offer funding for training to its network members. These can be great opportunities to find funding for relevant conferences or workshops that can build on subject expertise. However, there are some additional steps to consider. Particularly with government funding, there is often follow-up that needs to be performed as part of the award, such as writing a report on the activity. Make sure you thoroughly research to find out what the requirements are post-award. You want to ensure you stay in good standing so that you can be considered for future activities.

Other outside-of-the-box activities to find funding include looking for fellowship or grant opportunities. These are usually a bit harder to find but can offer longer-term learning experiences than some of the other forms mentioned. And of course, there is always self-funding to consider. No matter what funding route you decide to pursue, remember that the knowledge and experience gained is priceless when applied to your ultimate goal.

DOING THE TIME DANCE

I wanted to take a minute to loop back around and talk about finding the time to commit to learning, because, let's face it: making time for lifelong learning can sometimes be harder than actually figuring out what to learn next. Determining the right balance very much depends on your personal situation and learning plan. To build a truly sustainable plan will ultimately require some trial and error.

Below are some ideas you can adapt to your environment to make lifelong learning a priority:

- Create a workplace interest group around professional development that meets monthly. Each meeting could focus on a different topic or skill.
- Talk to your manager about lifelong learning, and try to determine a mutually agreeable learning schedule. This could be weekly, monthly, or yearly.

Top Five Behaviors to Help Cultivate Lifelong Learning

- Know that learning will happen whether we are aware of it or not—so be an active participant.
- Identify how you learn best.
- Approach everything with curiosity.
- Create a game plan on how you will prioritize learning regardless of what happens in the day to day.
- Advocate for your organization to adopt a culture of learning.

Top Five Behaviors to Avoid to Foster Lifelong Learning

- Procrastinating—true learning requires prioritization and attention
- Only updating current skill sets
- Thinking you're too new or too far into your career to be mentored
- Assuming you will find time to learn—make the time
- Trying to learn something that neither interests nor resonates with you

- Identify learning formats and content that can be consumed on the go; leverage that mobile device!
- Like exercise, explore learning in modular bites. Instead of watching an entire systematic review series in one sitting, spread it out over several days with an emphasis on taking time for implementation and reflection.

As with adding any new routine or priority, consistency is the key. Your learning may need to show up in creative or out-of-the-box ways. Let it. Lifelong learning is more about the commitment and effort to learn than the packaging of the content. In the end, sprints can be just as effective as marathons to getting you over that learning finish line. The "best" strategy is the one that works for you.

PARTING THOUGHTS

While lifelong learning has always been important for libraries, in today's world it is essential for survival. The rapid changes that are now part and parcel of everyday life will mean that current and future library professionals will need to bring their A game to every encounter. Life-

Action Items Recap

- Determine your educational end game.
- Spend some time investigating what funding you may have at your disposal.

long learning is our survival mechanism in the world of guerilla data and information warfare.

This new technological landscape has opened up the breadth and scope of not only what content is out there but also when and how we choose to learn. Unlike those before us, we now have the power to learn when, how, and where we want. But it is entirely up to us to commit to do the work in the midst of so many competing priorities. True powerhouse librarians know that regardless of the learning path, cultivating curiosity is an important attribute to successfully continuing the learning cycle. Let that curiosity burn bright and usher us into the next wave of librarianship fearlessly and freely.

REFERENCES

Gardner, Howard, and Thomas Hatch. 1989. "Multiple Intelligences Go to School: Educational Implications of the Theory of Multiple." *Educational Researcher* 18 (8): 4–10.

Herrmann, Esther, Josep Call, María Victoria Hernàndez-Lloreda, Brian Hare, and Michael Tomasello. 2007. "Humans Have Evolved Specialized Skills of Social Cognition: The Cultural Intelligence Hypothesis." *Science* 317: 1360–66.

McCue, T. J. 2014. "Online Learning Industry Poised for $107 Billion in 2015." *Forbes*, August 27. Accessed November 13, 2015. http://www.forbes.com/.

2

Taking the Plunge
The Benefit of Taking Risks

How This Might Look in Practice:

- Cultivate out-of-the-box relationships (e.g., theater department as a training partner to develop teaching presence).
- Experiment with building a taxonomy of hashtags.
- Launch an open-access interdisciplinary journal.

Everyone has needed to take a risk at some point in his or her life. It may have been big or small, and had minimal impact or a resounding ripple effect. Some risks may have garnered grand success, while others resulted in terrible failure. Each situation was likely unique but with two necessary commonalities. Someone needed to make a decision and get something done.

Risk is defined in *Merriam-Webster* as "the possibility that something bad or unpleasant (such as an injury or a loss) will happen." Getting results requires knowing when to take a risk and when to walk away. For some, the ability to be a risk taker comes more naturally. Looking at the research, some studies argue that certain personality types have a higher threshold to engage in risky behaviors (Highhouse and Yüce 1996). This threshold may initially make decision making easier for some individuals. However, this inclination is not necessarily a permanent hall pass. Other research suggests that risk taking may be influenced by a combination of internal and external factors (Weber and Milliman 1997). Although someone may be more naturally inclined to take a risk, these behaviors can be influenced by the likelihood of profit or loss, a phenomenon known as "prospect theory" (Kahneman and Tversky 1979). To further complicate matters, other influences such as sociopolitical factors, gender, race, past behavior, and perception may all play a role in a person's willingness to play the risk game (Nicholson et al. 2005). So where does all of this conflicting theory leave you, dear reader?

The hard reality is that for anyone (or any project) to be a success there is some level of risk taking involved. Very few (if any) powerhouse librarians accomplished their greatest achievements without being willing to put themselves out there in some way. Since the focus of this book is really on how to effectively get things done, we will be talking about risk taking in the context of innovation and projects. To be fair there are a number of other areas where risk can be introduced into a library. For additional thoughts on these areas, I've included examples and some potential strategies at the end of this chapter. The following sections are designed to help you assess when to take risks and, when you do put yourself out there, how to do so more successfully.

KNOW THYSELF

The most recent risk I took was to leave my last position where I had been for over eleven years. I had become very knowledgeable and skilled in that role. But another aspect of risk taking is to do an honest self-assessment to determine if you are doing your best work. Is your situation tapping into the best of you? Are there skills you would like to develop that are not part of your current position? Be prepared that you may come to answers that may make you uncomfortable, but discomfort is just part of the equation of risk taking. (GK)

There are any number of internal and external forces at work trying to influence your decision making on any given day. These forces, especially the external ones, can change frequently and disrupt our preferred method of handling things that are thrown at us. Knowing yourself is the first and most critical step to take in working to become a more effective library risk taker. Are you a free spirit who takes risks regularly? Do you prefer to stick to the same daily routine? Does change disrupt you to the core, or are you always looking for a way to shake things up? Having a clear understanding of where you naturally fall on the risk-taking scale is helpful in determining how much personal preparation you will need to do to feel comfortable taking risks. There are a number of free online tests you can take to determine your personal preferences. Below are a few simple questions you can ask yourself to start thinking about your stance on risk:

- When someone says the outcome is "unknown," how does this make you feel?
- How easily do I bounce back from "failures"?
- When doing something new, how do I usually approach things? Do I jump in or thoroughly research first?
- How likely am I to play games of chance, such as the lottery?
- If someone offered you the job of your dreams out of the blue, but you needed to relocate to a different city or country where you knew no one, and you only had forty-eight hours to decide, would you take it?

Based on how you responded to the above questions, you will likely have a good idea of how open you are to taking chances. If you found that you are fairly risk averse, don't worry. You are actually in pretty good company. Let's examine for a moment why this attitude seems to dominate.

Most of us live in a world where risk is the enemy and it must be avoided at all costs. For many, the word "risk" instantly conjures up images of loss, an automatic negative connotation. You may have even had a physical or emotional reaction just reading the word. Let's be honest. Most of us spend our time trying to minimize losing what we have. Librarians create archives and repositories, subscribe to a variety of resources, and figure out ways to continually rebrand our services. The most basic function of a library is to collect and provide access to a world of information. Much of our lives, both personal and professional, is spent acquiring; if you disagree, just look at the booming financial-planning section within your library's collection. So to purposely put ourselves, or our assets, on the line is a very uncomfortable scenario.

The need for comfort, both physical and material, is one of the driving forces of society today. According to Abraham Maslow, each individual has five innate needs. These needs are categorized as physiological, safety, love, esteem, and self-actualization (Maslow 1943). The idea of loss (and thus risk taking) at any of these levels poses a direct threat to our ability to fulfill these driving forces. This threat in turn creates one of the most primitive and effective feelings in the human spectrum of emotion: fear.

Fear is a fantastic inhibitor to action. Humans are chemically and physically wired to respond when the emotion strikes us—the classic fight-or-flight response. When we encounter a stimulus that can be perceived as a threat (from either past experience or having no frame of reference), the amygdala is flooded with chemicals creating the fear response. This innate response has been instrumental in keeping the human race alive for the past millennia. However, the inability to control this primal urge in the modern day can lead to all kinds of personal challenges—including relationship problems, communication breakdowns, and chronic health conditions.

Fear can be counterproductive in any area of our lives. However, fear in the workplace can directly impact not only our personal well-being but our financial success as well. In the workplace fear can be exhibited in a number of ways. According to Kathleen Ryan and Daniel Oestreich, authors of *Driving Fear out of the Workplace*, in recounting work done by S. J. Rachman, "'Fear can be acquired vicariously or by direct transmission of information. If in the face of threats, we feel unable to control the probable outcome, we are likely to experience fear.' Controllability is a key element from [Rachman's] perspective. He also finds that 'behavior or information that increases one's predictability is likely to contribute to a reduction in fear'" (Ryan and Oestreich 1991, p. 14). If you ever interact with other people regularly (and I'm assuming you do), then the above situation is an easy scenario to fall into. Even if you work in a happy-go-lucky, perfect organization, on occasion there is likely to be an information hiccup that causes at least mild anxiety—even in the most daring individual. So, assuming abandoning all society is not a realistic option, what can be done?

DEALING WITH THE FEAR FACTOR

The fear created from the discomfort associated with risk taking may be a very real obstacle in your path to successfully getting things done. Be-

---

Important Tip

Fear does exist for a reason. Always be sure to "gut check" your risk before moving ahead.

---

low are some easy, quick strategies you can implement to keep fear from sidetracking your project:

- Visualize the fully formulated end product. By focusing your attention on what you are hoping to accomplish, rather than on what can go wrong, you can redirect your energy to sleuthing out practical steps to make your end product a reality.
- Engage a trusted colleague. Sometimes you just need to get ideas out of your head. Discuss your fear with someone whose opinion you value to see if your concern is really warranted; then use your combined creativity to address any reality-based problems.
- Breathe. It's amazing the physical effect fear can have on the body. Take a few deep breaths to calm the nervous system and refocus as needed.
- Change your internal dialogue. If hearing the word *risk* automatically makes your palms start sweating, try finding a synonym that has a less intense meaning attached to it. For example, telling yourself you are taking a chance rather than a risk can reframe the experience in a more positive light. The word *chance* implies the same experience but is relatively neutral. You may also choose to use *challenge*, *innovate*, or *inspire*.

Knowing your tolerance for risk and how to deal with any fear is a necessary first step to develop your framework for success. Once this foundation has been determined you'll be ready to move on to developing a risk-oriented action plan.

CREATING A PLAN

Any powerhouse librarian who has successfully taken a risk most likely had a prerisk strategy in place. This plan should focus on not only defining and evaluating the risk but also behaviors or action items you can implement to reduce the likelihood of a negative experience. By adopting positive risk-taking behaviors before the project starts, you can better prepare for whatever result the experience produces. The following are some practical steps and attitudes you can adopt to begin developing your personal risk framework.

Think It Through

The first step you must take is clearly outlining the project from start to finish. You will not be able to effectively evaluate how much of a risk you are taking if the project itself is muddy. Brainstorming and storyboarding are two effective ways to create a holistic picture. However, as a best practice, you should create a formal written project proposal. I strongly encourage this—even if nobody else ever sees it. Getting your project onto paper is important for several reasons. Creating a proposal will

- force you to determine whether or not you feel strongly enough about the project to initiate the work necessary to carry it out (hint, hint: If you don't really want to do this step, the answer is probably no);
- keep all of the details straight and help determine a checklist to keep the project on track later on;
- give you a framework to make sure that as the project progresses, you are not starting to stray from the original scope and intent;
- show administrators you are serious about the project and are willing to think through all of the necessary details; and
- provide something solid for you to talk to colleagues and stakeholders about to generate needed buy-in.

A standard project proposal should include, but is not limited to, the following:

- Clearly define what the project is and what the outcome should be.
- List any actions or goals that are out of scope.
- Articulate a justification for why the project is needed.
- Consider who it will impact and how.
- Develop a list of stakeholders (both definite and potential).

Important Tip

Getting things done requires flexibility. So although it is important to develop a plan, be sure to allow yourself some wiggle room to make adjustments when necessary.

- Identify barriers to the project such as budget or personnel.
- Determine the time commitment and sustainability of the project (e.g., Is the project short or long term?).
- Inventory the assets at your disposal now and their stability for the life of the project.
- Set up a plan to evaluate the outcome and disseminate the results.

Some sample templates are included for you at the end of this chapter. Taking the time to think through the entire project will help you identify potential problems from the start and develop a strategy to address these issues early on. Although time consuming, creating a plan (even one that is ultimately unsuccessful) will help build your confidence as you work toward your powerhouse goal.

Know Your Reality

To effectively determine how much of a risk your project poses to the status quo (an essential insight), it's important to have a good assessment of your current situation. Like the project itself, not stopping to assess personal and environmental factors can introduce avoidable barriers down the road. Although these barriers may not derail the project entirely, they can sidetrack it by delaying timelines, impacting budgets, or going back to get required approvals. Having a clear idea of what red tape you need to clear first is paramount for success. If you are not sure where to begin, ask yourself some simple questions:

- Do I realistically have time to pursue this project and make it successful? Where will it fall on my list of priorities?
- Do I currently have the skills necessary to undertake a project like this?
- Will the culture I'm in embrace or hinder this pursuit? How can I sell it effectively?

Important Tip

When determining whether or not you can sell your idea to management, take time to brainstorm questions they might ask you. Having answers to the big questions will be important for getting approval. If you have too many unanswerables, you may have to spend some time rethinking your project before proposing it.

- Do I have the support of management? If not, is it possible to get it, and how quickly?
- Who will likely be on board, and who will I most likely need to convince?

Be sure to remove any emotion during this reflection process and really evaluate your situation for any red flags. Clearly seeing your reality will ultimately help you gauge your likelihood of success. It may even help you determine whether or not your project will be able to get off the ground, saving you time and frustration along the way. Becoming a powerhouse librarian means developing a sense of knowing when to hold, when to fold, and when to walk away.

Build Your Confidence

If you are new to risk taking, building up your confidence before launching your project will be vital to seeing your vision through. There are two simple ways to begin this process.

One easy strategy is to start taking mini risks daily. These do not need to be life-changing gambles. Small wins, such as speaking up in a meeting, volunteering for a new committee, or even changing your daily coffee order, can reinforce the positive growth experiences risk taking can provide. By accumulating frequent, small victories, you can begin to become more comfortable putting yourself outside of your comfort zone.

Important Tip

Be sure to write these mini wins down for later. We are much more likely to remember negative experiences then positive ones. Having a ready list of positive achievements you can quickly refer to will help take the sting out of any minor setbacks.

The second strategy you can try is to develop a positive internal dialogue around risk. Start by collecting words that will help you focus on the rewards that come with taking a risk. Words such as *innovation, growth, opportunity, exploration,* and *problem solving* can help sustain and refocus your attention when doubt or unexpected challenges arise. Cultivating a healthy outlook and vocabulary can also help you in marketing or selling your vision when needed later on.

Depending on your threshold for risk, building confidence may take time. It's important to view this step as a work in progress. You will likely have to challenge yourself to do these exercises over and over again. Taking risks may never be comfortable for you; however, you can definitely develop the confidence you need to persevere with the risks you do choose to take.

Redefine Success

One of the pitfalls to any project is predefining what success looks like. To many, success comes in the shape of a very specific form or outcome. We frame our endeavors by using an either/or vocabulary. The formula is simple: if I do x, and do it well, then I should get y result. Translation: Either I will be successful or I will fail.

Depending on your outlook, risk taking highlights this contrast and emphasizes the need to succeed for many. The tendency for most to see risk negatively magnifies the need to achieve x. We are conditioned to believe that if we perfectly execute the steps of our plan, then whatever we have identified as our outcome will naturally be the end result. Any other outcome equals failure. Wake up! It is now your job to see beyond the lure of this x effect.

True powerhouse librarians know that defining success as a single result limits their ability to be open to possibility. By focusing too much on one outcome, we become blind to the other options at our disposal. Too many people develop a mental narrative that must unfold in a specific way. They are stuck watching that same formulaic romantic comedy over and over again. You know the one: boy meets girl, boy gets girl, boy loses girl, boy gets girl again, and they both live happily ever after—the end. The problem with this framework is that it does not take into account the unpredictability of reality. Life is unpredictable—we know this!

Your goal is to think about success as a "choose your own adventure" story. Build in room for the unexpected plot turns before they turn into personal landmines. Here are some practical tips for redefining your take on success:

- Mentally create alternative endings. By creating multiple stories for what success looks like, you will help yourself to avoid becoming too attached to a single outcome. By detaching you will be more likely to see alternative possibilities you may have missed originally.
- View your project as a hypothesis. The truth is we always think we know what is going to happen, but rarely do we know for certain. By viewing the whole process as an experiment you may help yourself to be more objective and mentally trick yourself into not clinging to one success path.
- Rethink your views on failure. What actually is failure? According to the *Oxford English Dictionary*, failure is defined as (1) A lack of success, or (2) The neglect or omission of expected or required action. The keyword here for our purposes is expected. We view something as a failure when it does not meet the expected mental story we created. And since we internally determine our success story, we often personalize failure. What if we rewrote the story to frame failure as a way to get feedback? By viewing failure as a tool rather than an outcome, you can use it to achieve your redefined view of success.

Success really is an objective measure that can be molded to look anyway you see fit. Take advantage of this flexibility, and be open to capitalizing on any unexpected results that come your way. They may just be your ticket to bigger and better things.

An unexpected opportunity came my way when I was doing work as an outreach librarian for the National Network of Libraries of Medicine. One of the

Important Tip

Changing your way of thinking is a process and takes time. There are some really great books available on this topic. Check out the cognitive psychology section at your local bookstore.

states my office served is Montana. I had met one of the hospital librarians in Montana at a conference previously and was preparing to go to the Montana Library Association meeting that was taking place not too far from this gal's home. She asked me, "Would you like to go to a cattle-branding party?" How could I say no to an experience like this? Talk about the quintessential Montana activity! By taking the risk of saying yes, I got to see what life in Montana is like on a working ranch. It helped me understand the rich lives of people in Montana communities but also see some of the challenges they face: having to travel long distances to access health care; struggling to make ends meet when fuel prices skyrocket and they have to use trucks and farm vehicles on a daily basis; and the fact that there are very few medical libraries in the state of Montana for people to be able to access authoritative health information. By accepting this invitation, I was able to build a relationship with a valued colleague but also to build my credibility in a consulting role to others in the state of Montana because I had taken the time to experience life alongside them. (GK)

Being Open to Saying Yes

One of the best habits you can strive to develop is cultivating an open mind. Being willing to say yes is an essential practice among those who get things done. This practice applies to not only other people but yourself as well. That is not to say that yes should be your automatic answer to every request. Knowing when to say no is just as important. However, being willing to stretch in ways you never saw for yourself may lead to some surprising insights, as illustrated by the case above.

Five Good Risk-Taking Habits to Cultivate

- Risks should be calculated before any action is taken.
- Take time to question your motivation.
- Solicit input.
- Be prepared for outcomes to look different than you may have expected.
- Take time to reflect.

Five Risk-Taking Habits to Avoid

- Taking impulsive risks
- Disregarding or ignoring your current environment or situation
- Avoiding any external feedback
- Taking too many risks at once
- Not evaluating the outcome

Saying yes provides opportunities for growth as well as connection. These attributes are key drivers for any powerhouse librarian. The above experience is a perfect example of how a random, out-of-the-box opportunity provided unique insight that likely would never have been acquired otherwise.

Chances to grow are rarely premeditated. We never know which experience will lead to our next opportunity. Saying yes ensures that we are laying the groundwork and building the capacity to move forward toward a future laced with potential.

PARTING THOUGHTS

Risk taking is a necessity for those who want to get things done. Powerhouse librarians know how to leverage a risk to get the maximum benefit. Taking risks may not be natural for many of us, but working to develop some level of risk tolerance is imperative to creating new and dynamic opportunities.

Remember that risk taking is like a muscle that needs to be exercised. The more you work to develop it, the easier the experience will become. However, like any new skill, it is important to work on creating healthy habits while trying to avoid acquiring bad ones. Developing these habits will obviously not guarantee that every risk pays off but will hopefully help you avoid any pitfalls that are behavior related.

As you continue on your journey to becoming a powerhouse librarian, keep in mind the old adage "nothing ventured, nothing gained." The profession is drastically changing, and you have the opportunity to push it forward in directions we never dreamed of before. So be willing to risk being great.

Action Items Recap

- Spend time completing a self-inventory to determine your comfort with risk taking.
- Develop an assessment of your current culture and environment.
- Draft a project proposal that outlines the project in its entirety to help identify if this project is the proper risk for you.
- Create a personal plan to deal with uncertainty to mitigate any discomfort you feel from the process.

SAMPLE PROJECT PROPOSAL 1

Project Overview

Justification

Scope	Inside	Outside

Stakeholders	Internal	External

Impacts

Commitment and Sustainability

Evaluation Plan

Assets	Barriers

SAMPLE PROJECT PROPOSAL 2

Overview and Justification

In Scope

Outside Scope

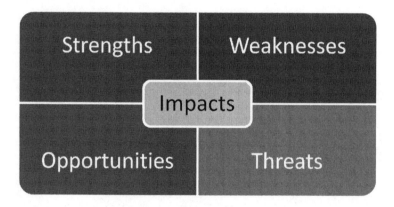

Stakeholder	Internal	External	Potential	Definite

Assets	**Needs**
1.	1.
2.	2.
3.	3.

Evaluation Plan

SAMPLE PROJECT PROPOSAL 3

Project Overview and Justification

Project Scope

Impacts and Outcomes

Stakeholders

Assets and Barriers

Future Considerations

Evaluation and Dissemination

Research (optional)

Examples of Library-Related Risks	Examples of Influential Forces	Sample of Potential Strategies
Changes happening at an organizational level	External or internal at the organizational level and likely to be at the leadership level	Keep meaningful metrics. Have both quantitative and qualitative data available to share with important influencers.
Implementing new services or revamping currently offered ones	External or internal at all levels from users to staff and administration within the organization	Gather data from a variety of sources both internally and externally. Build in feedback touchpoints throughout the process to make small redirects. Devise success metrics and plan review periods.
Making the move to digital (e.g., collection, space, etc.)	External or internal at the organizational level Technology Industry User based	Review and implement sound collection policies. Get a clear idea of user and administrative expectations. Involve both internal and external stakeholders throughout the process.
Expanding interprofessional roles within the library	External or internal at the organizational level	Communicate a solid vision for the position and how it relates to the larger mission and vision. Engage HR to learn best practices for recruitment, onboarding, teambuilding, etc.

REFERENCES

Highhouse S., and P. Yüce. 1996. "Perspectives, Perceptions, and Risk-Taking Behavior." *Organizational Behavior and Human Decision Processes* 65 (2): 159–67.

Kahneman, D., and A. Tversky. 1979. "Prospect Theory: An Analysis of Decision under Risk." *Econometrica* 47 (2): 263.

Maslow, A. H. 1943. "A Theory of Human Motivation." *Psychological Review* 50:370–96.

Nicholson, N., E. Soane, M. Fenton-O'Creevy, and P. Willman. 2005. "Personality and Domain-Specific Risk Taking." *Journal of Risk Research* 8 (2): 157–76.

Ryan, K., and D. K. Oestreich. 1991. *Driving Fear out of the Workplace: How to Overcome the Invisible Barriers to Quality, Productivity, and Innovation.* San Francisco: Jossey-Bass.

Weber, E. U., and R. A. Milliman. 1997. "Perceived Risk Attitudes: Relating Risk Perception to Risky Choice." *Management Science* 43 (2): 123–44.

3

Engaging Creativity
Dream, Build, Be

How This Might Look in Practice:

- Design library spaces that contain an element of surprise (e.g., painting a chalkboard wall versus installing a whiteboard).
- Create an employee event highlighting something unique about your library (e.g., transforming book carts into story characters).

Stop and ponder for a moment the following questions. What does it mean to be creative in modern society? Is there benefit to bringing creative practices into the workplace? How do we foster creativity within ourselves and those around us while still striving to get work done? If the answer seems immediately obvious to you, congratulations. You are likely way ahead of the game and setting your library on new pathways at this very moment. If you have never really given the topic much thought, take heart, you're not alone.

The questions above and many similar ones are beginning to become real, pertinent topics of conversation across industries and cultures. Libraries are no exception. In our world we use descriptors such as innovative, flexible, and adaptable as attributes we want to aspire to. But where do these benefits stem from? Creativity, according to *Merriam-Webster*, is the "ability to make new things or think of new ideas." The need for new is a pressure every librarian, new and seasoned, can relate to.

Changes within health care, higher education, industry, and government are impacting libraries at every level and causing us to ponder, *who are we?* Most of this is spurred by the lightning-fast changes in technology that are now part of our daily existence. But changes to funding structures and publishing models and shifts in cultural attitude all drive this conversation, often with very real outcomes for libraries forced to have those discussions at the request of external parties—cue the angsty music.

Before you get too depressed and decide to leave librarianship for a promising career as an analyst, broker, or some other up-and-coming data field, take heart. Salvation can be found and is available to you at no money down. The answer lies with your creative self. True powerhouse librarians know how to tap into their creative conscious and harness the potential it offers into viable solutions for our patrons. This chapter is designed to get you thinking about creativity and how you can use it to shape yourself and the library of the future. Be warned: talking creative is not for the faint of heart.

WHO IS CREATIVE

Often we identify the creative process with others. People such as artists, marketers, writers, and entrepreneurs are upheld as icons of what creativity should look like. Rarely do we give ourselves credit for the small flashes of brilliance we muster on a daily basis. Everyday creativity can surface in the form of problem solving, creation of a product, reconfiguring a schedule, or authentically recognizing someone for their actions.

Creativity is the one human gift that belongs to everyone. We naturally have varying levels of inherent talent, but I would argue that no one is entirely uncreative. Seeing yourself as a creative person can take time and practice. Like any ability, creativity requires commitment of personal resources such as time, attention, and desire. However, there are simple practices you can do to try to grow your natural creative talents.

Build in time for reflection and quiet. This doesn't have to be a big chunk of time out of your day. Simply setting aside ten minutes can be enough to clear out the white noise and help you connect to your creative self. We can't be creative if our attention is split between a million different tasks. Commit to the time to be present, open, and nonjudgmental.

Mind your self-talk. We all have a certain way we view ourselves. If getting in touch with your inner creative is a new experience for you, make sure you are aware of any negative self-talk you might be reinforcing. Remember, not every idea or output you produce will be brilliant. But "stepping stone" ideas always pave the way to "the one"—just ask any Microsoft, Apple, or Twitter innovator.

Find your tribe. Changes are always easier to facilitate when you have a support network around you. Why? Our tribes hold us accountable. They pick us up when we are wallowing. And sometimes creativity flows faster and freer when we have someone to bounce ideas off of. Finding a "buddy" works for lots of areas in our lives (hello workout partner!). The creative arena is no different.

Find the process that works for you. Creativity is about being authentic. Artists' work resonates with others because the song, painting, or poem is an extension of who they are. Find and adapt a creative workflow that fits your temperament and working style.

The beauty of being creative is that there is no market on possibility. There are many ways for creativity to show itself. Your opportunity is waiting. So jump in!

WHY DOES CREATIVITY MATTER

You might be thinking, What's with the sudden interest in matters of the creative mind? Why is everyone so focused on finding inspiration or being inspirational? I would urge you to look at the continual iterative changes happening within the sectors of industry and technology. Our economy is centered around "the next big thing." The move to "innovation" is a driving motivator for the majority of businesses, institutions, and products today. For many, the mantra is innovate or die (not really, but it can sure feel that way sometimes!).

Creativity matters because it is the defining force of innovation. If you don't believe me, just try and come up with a new angle to a library project or problem doing your normal, rote routine. Pretty hard, right? The creative mind is the platform from which solutions and new avenues present themselves. Without this key ingredient we become stuck in a cycle of cyclical thinking. What's the harm in that? Although there's no harm in the short term, if our social and professional capital is being defined by the new language of development, refusing to participate will cost us in the future. As the language of value morphs under the heightened pressure of "what's next," libraries run the risk of becoming obsolete. It's a painful truth, but it is true.

Building a culture and profession where creativity is the standard is our way to ensure that the value of libraries and librarians is recognized now and into the future. Creativity is the currency of the future. So what does this mean for you, the powerhouse-librarian-in-training? Keep reading to find out.

WHAT IS CREATIVE LIBRARIANSHIP

Creative librarianship takes many forms. We spend time building tax-onomies, designing flexible spaces, and developing services that serve a need or expectation of our users. Massages in the library anyone? As our users become more sophisticated in their tastes, so must we in the way we choose to respond. Capitalizing on our innate creativity is the key ingredient in ensuring we continue to serve the communities we engage with.

Any powerhouse librarian knows that gathering constructive feedback is essential for framing important conversations such as which new ser-vices to roll out. It is important to remember that as much as we need creative answers to our changing landscape, we need to base our creative endeavors on sound, documented need. Why? As in evidence-based medi-cine (shout out to any of you medical librarians reading out there), you need to incorporate the end user's values/desires into the mix. Without it, you can create the most groundbreaking new service, but it will likely go unnoticed because the audience doesn't need or want it. Game over. Project fail.

Important Tip

Evidence-based medicine is generally described as the interplay among the literature, patient desire, and the experience of the clinician. Without the patient's buy-in or practitioner's clinical expertise, the evidence (aka literature) goes unused. This can result in a number of outcomes, some not always positive.

Truthfully, I think that the library as place is the perfect launchpad for creative disruption. The uses people find for our spaces, resources, and services are imprinted throughout our culture in various ways. How many great authors, scientists, and educators have found solace and kinship within the confines of the library? What have those collaborations led to? We have always been a gathering place for those seeking to invent. How do we go about weaving that essence into our library practice? The answer lies in what your library is at its core.

To me, creative librarianship, and thus creative libraries, is about authenticity and embracing the changing landscape for what it is: an opportunity to continually redefine and share who we are while honoring our rich history of tradition. The process requires us to commit to always question and be willing to respond with an honest answer. It requires us to be brave.

I was recently asked to come up with ideas for pilot projects in rural outreach for our state. I did my own brainstorming to come up with a couple things I had been thinking about. Specifically, I suggested reaching out to groups of health-care professionals in the state who might need access to biomedical literature and clinical tools but didn't have the funding or the connections to get it. Then I started talking to other people. What do you think? And that added a collection of ideas, and their connections to people then led to other ideas that I wouldn't or couldn't have thought of. Our proposal is now a strong document with collaborative backing from various groups in the state to work together should funding be awarded. Had I not asked other people to chime in, this wouldn't be the powerhouse proposal it is now. (KT)

Creativity in our spaces can surface by telling our stories in new and interesting ways. It may spark from pairing up unusual combinations of folks to solve a problem. Librarians who are creative find a number of means to do the following:

- blend the old and new when it's appropriate;
- include diverse ways of thinking and multiple perspectives into their data gathering and practices;
- share their vision in a way where others can visualize it; and
- identify ways to motive themselves and others to do the mundane.

They see the path where others only see forest. Creative libraries and librarians embrace what is and make it into what they want it to be.

THE ARGUMENT FOR CREATIVITY VERSUS INNOVATION

At this point you might be evaluating the need for creativity in your library. If you have been a practicing professional over the last five plus years, it is likely that you have participated in a conversation surrounding the need to change. Shifting demographics, learning styles, user expectations, accessibility, policies, and funding models are defining the future realities of the library profession. In essence, the core of librarianship is still intact, but the way we execute those principles changes in radical fashion daily. It is no wonder that we are also feeling the push to brand ourselves as "innovative."

Innovation has become the new buzzword of Libraryland. If you don't believe me, take a look at a random sample of library missions, marketing materials, and job postings. See what I mean? The *I* word is everywhere! Now before you're too tempted to jump in and drink the innovation Kool-Aid, I'm going to ask you to stop and pause for a minute. Put down the Kool-Aid and back away. Why, you might be wondering? To me, and I would argue any true powerhouse librarian, we should be striving for the *C* not the *I*.

That's blasphemy, you might be thinking! I've been mandated to innovate. Innovation is where it's at. Just take a minute to hear me out. It is our creative selves that allow us to rethink, redesign, and dream up what is around the corner. Creativity allows us to learn how to flex. If you don't commit to developing alternative frameworks, thinking patterns, or methodologies, then innovation cannot happen. Innovation is the byproduct of a creative environment.

According to the *Oxford English Dictionary*, the origin of the word *innovate* stems from Latin: *innovare*, which roughly translates into "making new," and surfaced during the sixteenth century. This makes sense given that this was the time period where humanity was making giant steps forward in terms of exploration and discovery. Not only were ideas being pondered, but also we were actually acting on those ideas and desires to create things the world had yet to see.

As we ponder how to redefine ourselves, I would urge librarians at every level, particularly those of us in leadership, to focus on building our creative collateral rather than expending energy getting our users to see us as innovative. I know this is a shift away from today's popular thinking. However, I would argue from personal experience and observation that our greatest role is to serve as the springboard for others' innovation. Our users are asking us to be flexible, responsive, and present partners. We succeed when we reflect back to them an understanding of who they are and what they need from us.

At this point you are probably thinking, "But we are providing things like our collections in electronic format, and circulating tablets for patron use. These things are innovative." For argument sake, to some degree you are right. But who drove those changes, and how did they come about? Shifts in consumer wants, technology, and publishing models gave rise to e-books. We circulate tablets because patrons like these technologies and are interested in using them. The library did not "create" these models or technologies. They exist outside of us. We were just smart enough to recognize their value (go us!). We are adapting, reflecting, and making accessible innovations that already exist. We are creatively using the core library principles of collections and circulation to meet stakeholder demand. It's the same thing we have always done; the packaging is just slightly different. And this is okay. Why? Collecting, instructing, serving, and being accessible is the library being authentic, and people like authenticity.

The next time you are directed to be innovative, I encourage you to stop and really reflect on what you are actually trying to accomplish. Does the moment really require true innovation, or are you looking at an opportunity for creative action? If you're not sure, below are some examples I would classify as creativity over innovation:

Example: Developing a Game to Teach Information Literacy

Innovation = Concept of gaming
Creativity = Utilizing a game to teach a topic not generally considered fun

Example: Creating a Mobile Optimized Schematic of Your Stacks to Locate Items

Innovation = Technology that responds to mobile devices
Creativity = Using said technology to make things easier to find for your patrons by not having to scroll all over a large map on their phone

Example: Providing Electronic Reference Services

Innovation = Development of new formats such as instant messaging and SMS

Creativity = Libraries realizing patrons might want to contact us using those methods

Powerhouse librarians know how to leverage outside innovations to make our facilities and services better. It is this creative reappropriation and adaptation that will allow libraries to truly excel.

BUILDING A CREATIVE CULTURE

It is easy to say we want to support creativity in our spaces and workers. But how do we actually go about building a creative culture? To start, you need to assess the reality of the current organizational culture. Organizational culture is as much a part of your library as is any staff member. This unseen force subtly (and sometimes not so subtly) influences what and how things get done; the way individuals relate to and interact with one another; and the speed at which initiatives move, in addition to a whole myriad of other more complicated factors. In discussing innovation in the workplace, the article "Developing the Creative Spark" notes that "employee perception of their workplace environment can impact on the generation and implementation of ideas" (2014, p. 5). It is no secret that the stimuli we experience every day can influence our internal and external outputs. Whether hospitable or hostile, we absorb the world around us in little ways we may not even be aware of, subtly influencing what we put back out into the world.

Building a culture of creativity will require conscious effort. The commitment will need to be reflected in not only the cultural attitudes presented by every individual within the library but also the organization's policies and practices. Creativity must be championed through all ranks. Failure to fully integrate into any one corner can easily derail the cultural transformation you are trying to create.

Any successful metamorphosis will require reinforcements. To generate lasting change will require sustained energy and attention; more than one person can give it. Therefore, it will be important for you to flex the powerhouse skill of empowerment. Empowering individuals to help lead this organizational revolution is necessary for long-term success. This is a crucial step because it ensures that colleagues feel invested in making the change happen, an immeasurable asset for when the road gets rocky. This step can take many forms. I have found that people generally like titles. It somehow makes their participation feel official. Identifying "creativity ambassadors" could be a fun way to bestow power to the effort's biggest cheerleaders. Look for individuals who really believe in what you are doing, and have them help you blaze the creative path.

On a more long-term front, your organization may consider adding creativity to the hiring criteria. A simple way to do this is to include a standard creativity question. By showcasing the organization's commitment to creative practice you are highlighting from the onset the expectation for creative, flexible thinking. Not only is this a potential recruitment tool for future hires, but also it ensures that the culture that you are working so hard to create will be sustained well into the future. Once established as the norm, depending on how your library operates, creative contributions could be built into the annual evaluation and merit criteria. Imagine the motivation to flex those creativity muscles then!

Finally, outside of building standard practices to support a culture of creativity, focusing on developing mechanisms to recognize and reward creative undertakings is an important component to establish. We have a bad habit of only heralding wild successes. Sometimes there is just as much honor in the efforts someone undertook to try to accomplish something. There are a myriad of reasons for why a project did not succeed. But that does not mean that the time, energy, and attention that a colleague or team poured into that effort are any less valuable than our big wins. Building systems to honor and appreciate the risks that one takes is a sure signal that your organization is living its commitment to the process.

Important Tip

Always consult with your human resources office on any new approaches related to hiring. They are a wealth of information and can help guide you through the process.

CREATIVE PRACTICES AT WORK: PRACTICAL STEPS

Finding time for creativity during the hustle and bustle of everyday business operations can be a challenge. Demands can be great, and the stress of putting out fires can easily usurp any extra time and energy found during the day. Therefore, it is imperative to find ways to build creativity outlets into the work environment.

Finding solutions to building a more creative-friendly environment doesn't need to be complicated. Sometimes the simplest solutions can be the easiest to maintain. But how will you know what solution will work for your environment? You need to begin by assessing not only the space but also resources and culture. To begin, you will want to spend some time doing the following:

Engage in employee conversations. Taking the time to incorporate the feedback from others cannot be overstated. This can be formal or informal. You may want to start out with a brief survey, focus group, or general discussion at an all-staff meeting. The format for gathering input can be varied, but investing the time to know how and what motivates and inspires your particular library "family" is essential for success.

Go for diversity. Focus on building a system that has a variety of options available to spark the creative mind. This will help to stymie boredom and also account for the unique needs of individuals. By having alternative activities and avenues for people to choose from, you can limit the time and energy folks have to waste thinking up an activity to pursue. You can also switch tactics easily if your go-to strategy fails to inspire.

Keep it fresh. Be prepared to build in flexibility and change into your process. These can be small, but continually making minor adjustments ensures that you are less likely to become stuck in routine. Comfort is a major derailer of creativity.

By taking a multipronged approach that is informed by your unique environment and is designed to be continually revised, you are creating a solid foundation for success. Now that you have your arsenal of information, you can begin examining your environment.

Creativity needs several elements to grow and take root. Designing spaces as well as practices that are conducive to the creative process are fundamental pieces to the puzzle. Imagine a time when you felt your most creative. Think about the surroundings. What do you notice about the physical space around you? How might that be different and possibly reproducible? The library environment we are in colors our internal landscape. Just as we impact the world around us, the surroundings we are in emit similar vibes that we absorb. Sounds silly, I know. However, how often have you had the experience of being somewhere and feeling one way and then changing locations and suddenly feeling different?

The energy in a space has to be right to allow the freedom for creativity to unfold. If you are stuck in a gray, isolated cubicle, the opportunity for inspiration is likely to be relatively limited. Now I could be wrong, and this might work for you. But call me crazy, I just don't see prison-chic really delivering the type of inspiration we are after. When you look around your space, if the words that are coming to you as descriptors are words like basement, confined, old, windowless, and so forth, take heart. There are lots of simple things that you can do to encourage a more creative friendly space. Regardless of your library type, a few of the following options may be easy to establish without much effort or cost:

- Display local or community art that rotates on a regular basis.
- Use discarded books or journal covers to create neat literary wallpaper or framed hanging art.
- Purchase colorful pillows that can be swapped out among furniture and spaces.
- Play soft background music as white noise.
- Bring in faux or real plants.
- Find and display quotes that inspire.
- Paint a wall with chalkboard paint to use for notes, murals, positive feedback, and so forth.
- Infuse color where you can.
- Reduce clutter to create more openness.
- Bring inside elements of nature, such as shells or stones you can use as connections to the outside world.

The list could go on and on. Infusing dynamic life into a space creates a connection. Feeling connected gives a sense of direction for your creativity to flourish. Now that we have our space squared away it is time to focus on creating creative practices.

Now this is where you can really start to have fun. The thing to take away from this last sentence is the doing. Creativity is ACTION. In her concise overview of creativity in the workplace, Fiona Powell shares insights from four creative specialists. According to James Hurman, author of *The Case for Creativity*, the best way to get the most creativity out of people is to follow the 10/90 rule. Only 10 percent of your time should be spent discussing things. The rest is devoted to actually doing it (Powell 2014/2015). The power of creativity is in the production. How often are you struck by creative insight when you're just sitting around zoned out? I'm guessing the answer is almost never.

True powerhouse librarians know there is power in doing (you will hear this a lot in this book). When it comes to inspiring creativity though, the trick is to balance action while staying open. In other words find an activity that engages you but not to the point you become so absorbed you shut everything else out. As you are designing your creative practices, remember to keep in mind that these processes don't all have to revolve around tangible activities. Some great creativity inspiring outlets could be

- protecting work time to pursue pet projects;
- holding walking meetings or moving meetings to an outdoor space;
- engaging in coloring, building clay sculptures, or doing some madlibs before a brainstorming session;
- developing an employee game collection that can be used during breaks or meetings;
- creating a monthly learning activity centered on talents or interests of employees; or
- sharing inspiring TED talks on a regular basis.

The avenue can be very different as you can see, but every activity requires action on the part of the participants. This activity is a catalyst for engagement. Engagement leads to connection. Connectedness sets a direction. All of these things are the breeding grounds for creativity and ultimately responsiveness and innovation.

Five Habits for Success to Cultivate

- Find champions at all levels to help build and sustain the culture.
- Find what works for your particular environment.
- Build creativity into your processes where applicable.
- Approach both success and failure from a place of curiosity.
- Commit to action.

Five Habits to Avoid

- Approaching creativity as a "one size fits all" process
- Implementing change for change's sake
- Setting unrealistic expectations (e.g., expecting every idea to be brilliant)
- Negative self talk
- Believing creativity belongs to only an elite few

PARTING THOUGHTS

In the race to survive and thrive in the modern world, the ability to morph, adapt, and change directions is an essential piece to remaining relevant. Through providing service in a world where technical and cultural disruption is the norm, creativity is the transformative force poised to help libraries transform into our next iteration.

By focusing on creativity rather than innovation, we can grant ourselves the freedom to stay true to what the library is at its core but reimagine ourselves to be who our constituents need and want us to be. Cultivating creative environments and mind-sets allows us to continually adapt at the rapid pace of the world today. True powerhouse librarians know how to harness their own creativity and fan the creative spark in others. So embrace your inner creative and lead by example. Your leadership may very well help to change the library world.

Action Items Recap

- Identify activities that naturally tap into your creativity.
- Build a regular time into your day to take a creativity break.
- When feeling blocked, move!

REFERENCES

"Developing the Creative Spark: Identifying Factors that Facilitate Innovation."
2014. *Strategic Direction* 30 (5): 4–6.

Powell, Fiona. 2014/2015. "Developing Creativity in the World of Work." *New
Zealand Management* 61 (5): 24.

4

Connecting Your Space and My Space
Growing Your Social Network

How This Might Look in Practice:

- Throw a speed-dating-style networking event hosted by the library.
- Develop communities of practice around interests as well as roles.
- Hold formal roles within local, regional, or national professional organizations.

In today's interconnected world, our successes rarely happen purely because of our individual efforts. Gone are the days of the lone wolf. Instead, today, success depends on our ability to meet, connect with, and leverage all of the resources at our disposal, in the right order at the right time, particularly when it comes to people. True powerhouse librarians know that growing your social network is one of the single most important things you can do career wise. Why? The vast majority of opportunities, resources, or signoffs you need to get things done come from knowing someone—or, more likely, knowing someone who knows someone (cue the ubiquitous "I know a guy, who knows a guy" movie scene here).

The modern world is all about connections. Where our networks used to be small, localized, and intimate, the advent of the Internet created the ability and need to influence across the bounds of space, time, and country. In a nutshell, the world exploded. We went from only having to flex our influence in our own small personal library sphere to suddenly needing to translate that same influence on a much larger, grander scale to effect change. We can still be agents of change within our institutions, communities, and so forth, but how often do we find ourselves needing to connect in order to learn how to move forward with x?

The need to know how to do something better, faster, or novel comes steeped in the desire to find information sources (aka people) who might have some insight and guidance in this area. Having a strong professional network provides ready access to a slew of knowledgeable resources saving you time, money, and sometimes a whole lot of failure—a fact that cannot be overlooked or overstated in the face of the rapid-pace changes happening today. As Kaisa Still, Jukka Huhtamaki, and Martha Russell (2015) note in their work on relational capital, "Increasingly, it is recognized that sustainable innovation activities—and other business activities—rarely are carried out by a single individual or within a single organization" (14). This is an eloquent description of our symbiotic library lives. Simply put, at a broader level, innovation and getting things done doesn't happen in a vacuum.

So what is a network, and how do we build one? First, let's tackle the network question. According to *Merriam-Webster*, networking is "the exchange of information or services among individuals, groups, or institutions; specifically: the cultivation of productive relationships for employment or business." Networking is the development of relationships, period. We have a variety of networks happening within our lives at any given time. They can be personal, professional, community, or faith based. Sometimes members of our networks intersect, making for deeper, more interesting exchanges (think the friend/library colleague experience). Social networks are our capital for getting things done. How we go about mindfully building them is as unique and varied a process as the library profession itself. The following are some strategies you can try to help grow your connections both in person and virtually.

Important Tip

Strong networks are created by building connections across disciplines, ranks, and interests *not* by targeting known names. Remember you never know who the next up-and-comers are going to be. Network and act accordingly.

WORKING THE CONFERENCE CIRCUIT

Attending professional meetings is a great opportunity to expand your professional network. Not only are they forums to stay current and learn about new trends in the field, but also I daresay 99 percent of conferences have networking opportunities built right into the program. Descriptors for these types of events to watch out for include the following:

- Anything "new member" related
- Welcome reception
- Closing reception
- Poster session
- Business lunch
- Roundtable discussion
- Tour
- "Vendor-hosted" x
- Exhibits

The true strength of conferences lies in the connections made both formally and informally. Most conveners know that, hence the wealth of opportunities to meet one another. New attendees or members networking with seasoned organization members bring new life into the group via membership, committee participants, potential collaborations (read future presentations), and vendor exhibition and sponsorships (important business networking for those collections folks). Although the content is an important draw for any meeting, the opportunity to network within the library or subject discipline community is a very close second. Occasionally, this can be more appealing than the content itself!

Using your time to network wisely at meetings is a skill most powerhouse librarians have learned to develop. Now let's be clear. Networking effectively doesn't necessarily mean that you know every single person in the room, although there are some natural networkers gifted enough to pull that off. Effective networking means you are present and attentive when you meet someone naturally and that you usually have an idea of one or two new people you would like to try to meet over the course of the conference. These can be people you've only met virtually, names you've seen on the listserv, or idols you've only read about in *Library Journal*.

Attending an in-person conference is the perfect time to solidify those connections to take them from nonexistent or fleeting to solid and lasting.

Okay, you're now convinced that attending the annual conference is a must for your professional (and little black book) development. But there's one problem: the agenda is jam-packed and you only know a handful of people going. How can you make sure you maximize your time effectively? Start by doing a bit of planning pre-event. The easiest place to get started is by reviewing the meeting guide. This will allow you to not only determine which sessions you might be interested in attending for the content but also identify new potential contacts in your areas of interest or specialty. Perusing the presenter list not only helps you plan your time wisely but also can offer up a great icebreaker if you need one during the conference. Starting a conversation with "I saw your presentation today" or "I noticed you're scheduled to give a talk tomorrow on X" rarely leads to the cold shoulder. Additionally, this can be a great tactic for those of us who might be more on the shy (or—GASP—awkward) side of the social spectrum. By leveraging the bits of info provided from the conference materials, you have an automatic opener not only to start the conversation but to put the other person in the lead role. Most people are excited to share their work with folks who have a genuine interest. So, as long as you are willing to ask questions, appear interested, and share bits of info back when asked, you're already set up for a winning conversation.

Aside from preplanning, multiday meetings can be a great way to leverage your preexisting contacts. Not only is this a great time to catch up socially and potentially plan new library projects, but also making new connections through existing ones is the fastest and easiest way to grow your social network. Think of it as the professional "six degrees of

---

Important Tip

When deciding to speak with people after their presentation, make sure you're mindful of their time. If the presenters you want to speak with have a line of people also eager to pick their brains, express your interest in their work, note the "competition," and offer to follow up by e-mail. This can be a great way to get you on their initial radar and gain contact information for follow-up. WARNING: Should you take this tactic, make sure you actually follow up the encounter with an e-mail! If not, you run the risk of looking disingenuous—definitely not the impression you want to make.

Kevin Bacon." This type of networking is indispensable for a number of reasons. For starters, all the players are "vetted." Most people we choose to network with we like to some degree or at the very least respect. That means that by scoring an introduction through an acquaintance or friend both parties already have insta-credibility. Additionally, these types of introductions often happen more organically, which can be very helpful for those of us who are more anxiety prone. Since the individuals doing the introducing know all parties involved, it's likely they'll provide connecting information right off the bat rather than make you have awkward small talk to find commonalities. This is a big win for those of us who find networking really hard or just downright terrifying.

On the flip side, it's more important that you bring your A game to these kinds of meetings. Why? Both your contact's and your social capital is on the line. If they go out of their way to introduce you and you behave poorly, the damage lands not only on you but on your contact as well. Not only is there a risk to that current relationship, but it also becomes unlikely your contact will be willing to do any future introductions. You just killed two potential networking avenues with one poorly aimed stone. Game over.

Although manners can never be overstressed, nowhere is this more true than in the contact introduction. So go forth and use this power wisely!

BUILDING A COHORT THROUGH WORKSHOPS, ACADEMIES, AND PROFESSIONAL ORGANIZATIONS

Like conferences, utilizing other venues such as classes can be a great way to add library colleagues to your contact list. This can be a solid strategy—particularly if you are participating in anything for an extended period of time. Participating in workshops or academies where you are part of a cohort immersed in learning creates a unique opportunity to bond not often found in the average one-shot training.

Part of the difficulty in networking is the necessity to engage an unknown agent. Finding ways to connect without really having an idea of whom you're trying to connect with can be challenging (or even terrifying) for sure. This shared experience offers an instant platform to begin moving beyond small talk into real, meaningful exchanges. Everyone is there for a similar purpose (although their circumstances may be different), which

Important Tip

Sincerity is an extremely important part of networking. Nothing will turn an interaction sour faster than coming off as a social climber or wannabe. Being sincere, genuine, and present in your interactions are sure steps to cultivating a positive impression.

gives you a built-in opening to work with. Additionally, leveraging the time factor also allows you more chances to establish relationships with more individuals. Where a daylong class might allow you to connect with the table you sat down with, attending a weeklong (or longer) training gives you the space to try to engage with a more diverse group of attendees.

However, you can make shorter experiences a successful networking opportunity as well. All the same benefits apply; it is just likely you will have less time to meet and try to connect with multiple people. For these networking sprints, establishing a memorable, positive connection is more important than meeting everyone in the room. Why? People remember how you made them feel, period. If you're so focused on trying to get through meeting everyone that the people you are talking to start to feel unimportant and blown off or that you're just schmoozing, that negative feeling is likely to stay with them, and you're metaphorically dead in the water. Now you might be thinking, "Come on, it can't be that bad. You can always make a comeback, right?" Maybe, but it's not likely.

Psychological studies have shown that negative events or emotions are easier for people to recall then positive ones. In their research on the power of good and bad, Roy Baumeister and his colleagues hypothesize that "it is evolutionarily adaptive for bad to be stronger than good. We believe that throughout our evolutionary history, organisms that were better attuned to bad things would have been more likely to survive threats and, consequently, would have increased probability of passing along their genes" (Baumeister et al. 2001, 325). In a nutshell, we're wired to be sensitive to bad experiences. Looking at it from a developmental standpoint, this rationale makes a lot of sense. That "ugh" feeling we experience is our internal alarm system keeping us safe. It guides us to bypass whatever danger we might be encountering (whether real or perceived). Avoiding unpleasantness means we get to stay in our happy, carefree bubble uninterrupted. Who doesn't want that?

Now if the evolution factor doesn't quite float your boat, another reason negative experiences might carry so much weight is due to the way the brain processes such experience. As Baumeister and colleagues explain, "In general, and apart from a few carefully crafted exceptions, negative information receives more processing and contributes more strongly to the final impression than does positive information" (Baumeister et al. 2001, 323–24). In theory this idea of cognitive processing time makes a lot of sense. If we spend more of our energy and attention identifying and evaluating what triggers a negative response, then that experience has more opportunity to become engrained on our psyche—good for biology, bad for you. Make sure you take the time to set a positive tone and make a good first impression, even if it means you do less networking. Having a single positive interaction will be a better advantage to you in the long run than having a handful of lukewarm or negative ones.

So how do we make speed-networking work to your advantage? Again, we do so by going back to knowing what you want to accomplish ahead of time. If you set a realistic goal (e.g., make one new contact) and a stretch goal (e.g., make three new contacts), then you can limit the pressured feeling that our overambitiousness can sometimes produce. Rather than feeling the minutes ticking away, you know that even if you only speak to one person, you've already succeeded and anything beyond that initial contact is a bonus. Repeat after me: quality not quantity.

The power of inclusivity can also be a strength in this situation. Sometimes we might dismiss opportunities to network with potential connections we've already made because we define who we "should" be networking with too narrowly. For instance, it can be just as valuable spending time talking to someone from systems who is sitting next to you, as it is to your fellow liaison librarians who are across the room. Why? Sometimes we're tackling the same problems from different perspectives or, more importantly, sometimes these folks can be impartial sounding boards for how to approach new contacts or stakeholders at your institution. Let me illustrate with a very simple and common library scenario:

Dana is fresh out of library school and got a job as a solo hospital librarian. She is working on purchasing new resources for the library, including several journals that provide useful video content. However, due to network security concerns, IT blocks videos from popping up on the network. These videos are high quality and will no doubt be useful to multiple users across the hospital. They cannot be removed from the package or hidden by the vendor. Both parties are concerned about access but from very different viewpoints. Dana has to decide by the end of the year whether or not she will purchase this package.

Knowing the right approach to take in this situation is critical to Dana's success. If Dana chooses only to surround herself with contacts who don't speak, understand, or care about technology, she is likely to miss out on simple language tweaks she can make to her exemption plea, tweaks that will likely resonate more with IT-oriented folks and are tantamount to her successfully solving her dilemma. Although it might be more comfortable to talk to someone who is a carbon copy of ourselves, the benefits of going outside our comfort zone are well worth the potential outcome.

NETWORKING BEYOND THE LIBRARY

To this point we've mainly focused on building your library or info-professional Rolodex. However, it is just as important to look beyond your current connections to the world outside of libraries. True powerhouse librarians recognize the insight and value nonlibrarian contacts can add to their own perspectives. Why, you might be wondering? As in talking to librarians who work in systems, knowing others in tangentially or even completely unrelated fields can shed light on solutions or problems we're grappling with in new and unexpected ways. Diverse perspectives breed better solutions. If that answer doesn't quite convince you, there is another bigger-picture reason interprofessional connections can be beneficial. It gets librarianship on other people's radar! And elevating our visibility in today's Internet age should be top priority. If people don't know what we bring to the table, they won't miss it when it's gone.

Interprofessional networking can be one of your best strategies to avoiding what I like to think of as the "(wo)man behind the curtain" syndrome. We as a profession are naturally committed to making our systems and services work as seamlessly as possible. That commitment is one of the things I admire most about librarians and is probably one of our greatest strengths. But pair that efficiency with a natural inclination to keep a low profile, and our professional and organizational visibility drop way down. That often puts the library in the danger zone. The more effectively we can network with our interprofessional colleagues, the more advocates we can cultivate to articulate our value. But where do we begin?

It starts by getting out of the library. One of the most effective moves a powerhouse-librarian-in-training can make is to join activities that happen beyond our walls. These could materialize as task forces, meetings, grand rounds, university committees, board meetings, product groups, and so forth. The list goes on and on.

Part of being visible in a meaningful way is to understand how your skills benefit the other players at the table. It is critical to know this because—by no fault of their own—your nonlibrary colleagues will likely perceive what you do in a very traditional way. It's all about those books, right? To be most effective in your networking, your next step is to talk to these interprofessional peers and find out about them. If you don't know what they do and have some idea of how they do it, your ability to contextualize your skills and modern librarianship will suffer. Good networking starts with them—not you! Once you have an idea about their interests or pain points, only then can you really connect your skill set in a valuable way.

A quick word of caution. If you want to communicate your value, it is imperative to know what the currency is. Like actual monetary currency, all people will have a different value system they find important for their job or profession. Talking to a chief financial officer (CFO) is very different than the junior faculty member in art history. Skip this step, and your new connection can go from promising to DOA fast. As when networking with other librarians, approaching new interprofessional colleagues with authenticity and curiosity is important to establishing a real connection.

In addition to getting out of the library and spending time learning about those you're networking with to enhance your impact, it is also important to be mindful about how you speak to them. And I'm not necessarily talking about tone, inflection, personal distance, and so forth. Rather, when first making a connection it's really important to avoid jargon or "librarianese" if you will.

Few people will understand terms such as taxonomy, interlibrary loan (ILL), metadata, or Boolean. These are things they may use on a regular basis but will likely not recognize in conversation. For instance, they might know that the library can get them articles from other places. However, they may not know that as head of ILL you oversee the article service. To effectively network it will be important to share your role, skills, and organization in clear, transparent language. By making sure you present yourself in an easily accessible way, you invite the nonlibrarians you are connecting with to see parallels between skills, responsibilities, interests, and so on. Below are a few tips on how to keep the jargon monster at bay:

- Avoid acronyms.
- Keep explanations simple.
- Clearly define any jargon you must use.

Learning to communicate jargon free (or jargon lite) has applications far beyond just networking. It can also help improve instruction, library marketing, and those elevator speeches true powerhouse librarians have crafted and ready to go.

Interprofessional networking is an important skill in your powerhouse arsenal. Learning to use it effectively can secure positive benefits at the personal and organizational level. Neglect it and your chances of "getting things done" will quickly disappear.

USING THE NET

Utilizing social media and other web technologies is a must-have skill for any powerhouse librarian. With the increased access to everything thanks to mobile technologies, we now have the opportunity to connect anytime, anywhere. Having a thoughtful online presence is quickly becoming necessary to stay connected in this brave new world. That is not to say that you must live and breathe the social media circuit, but knowing how to effectively leverage social media tools to market your library and yourself is critical to your growing network. Why? Your online presence may be the first time someone ever lays eyes on you. What story do you want your profile to tell?

The way you present yourself online will send a strong message, whether you intend it to or not. We are all humans and therefore multifaceted and deeply complex. Unfortunately, social media and the Internet don't necessarily capture the layered, nuanced, complicated us. They only capture what we feed it. That's why paying attention to your audience is an incredibly important part of online networking. How you choose to engage with and respond to things on social media creates a story around your identity. It is important to remember that although the computer screen can feel intimate and closed, the world beyond it is vast and deep. The person you blast on that professional listserv today can easily reemerge in the form of a potential reviewer, future colleague, or even a new boss. Unbecoming behavior can last a lifetime on the Internet. So it's incredibly important to be mindful about what you're floating to the world (at least in a professional context). Below are a few simple tips to help you either start or rethink your professional online presence.

Consider Keeping Your Personal and Professional Profiles Separate

This tip can be tricky but is something worth considering depending on your social media habits and personal comfort level. Some people decide to use different platforms for work and personal (think LinkedIn versus Facebook). Juggling multiple platforms can be time intensive but can help you clearly delineate professional and personal boundaries. And let's be clear, these boundaries are necessary to varying degrees. Although it's important to show your humanity in order to create meaningful connections, choosing to be completely unfiltered with the entire world 24/7 may have effects you haven't previously considered, particularly if you have a habit of accepting any contact request that comes your way. Case in point, I doubt that awesome profile picture showcasing your ability to rock a holiday onesie will be a high priority for the search committee members of that library director position you applied for. Context is everything! What looks fun and whimsical in one context may not carry the same message in another. It's important to realize that even if you create different accounts, there may be times when parties stumble upon your "other" profile. That is why the following is an important consideration.

You Have Privacy Settings for a Reason; Use Them

Most social networking platforms allow you to customize your profile settings to display as much or as little as you want to share. Spend the time to learn how to use these options. If you prefer to keep things totally open, explore your options of segmenting your contacts into specialized groups (e.g., work contacts and friends). Oftentimes you can set varying permission levels based on a contact's grouping. Although it is totally within your right to chronicle your every move, again try to be mindful of your audience. There is no legitimate reason the dean of your library, CEO of the company, or your library branch manager needs to know what you had for breakfast. Period.

You Are a Brand; Act Accordingly

You are your most valuable asset. The reputation you create for yourself will stay with you throughout your professional life. Make sure the content you put out there reflects that. The words we choose, pictures we post, things we share, people we follow, and conversations we engage in all paint a picture of who we are. It's important to remember that the world may not have the benefit of knowing all the cosmic inner workings that contributed to that random rant you tweeted at 2:00 a.m. Make sure to think twice before hitting that post button.

> The organizations and individuals I've observed having the greatest success have some common attributes: clear social media policies so that all who are posting are "playing by the same rules"; regular and frequent posting; the willingness to take risks at times and post things that are genuine and authentic, even if they're not going to be in agreement with the "majority"; and lastly an overall positive and professional tone to the posts. When people are enthusiastic about the topics about which they are posting, it is very apparent. When posts are just "plain vanilla," well, that's obvious too. (GK)

As with so many other things in life, taking time to really reflect on how you want to present yourself online cannot be emphasized enough. Your profile is your unofficial digital résumé in a lot of ways. It may not be the thing that lands you that job, project, or contract. However, it certainly helps shed light on what you value, like, dislike, your personal outlook, and so forth. The same care and attention should be taken to ensure it accurately reflects you—a unique blend of fun, thoughtfulness, and professionalism.

MANNERS MATTER

As William of Wykeham famously declared all the way back in the thirteenth century, "manners maketh man" or—in the case of many librarians—woman. The power and influence of manners cannot be overlooked when considering how to grow your social network. How we present ourselves and behave have a direct impact on the success of our connections. Manners, or a lack thereof, are one of the few facets of relationship building that are directly within our control. Therefore, it makes sense to spend some time polishing these skills as early on in your career as possible. The rules of proper etiquette are far too nuanced and numerous to adequately be covered here. In fact, it would be silly to even try. However, there are a few simple things that any powerhouse-librarian-in-training can start doing to build a positive and lasting impression.

For starters, taking the time to learn proper dining etiquette is a skill that will never go to waste. Now you might be thinking, "wait a minute, in my library the only person who would need to have fancy dining skills is my manager/director/dean/." And to some extent that might be true. Depending on your job, it's unlikely that you will need to pull this skill out on a regular basis. However, the times you do utilize it will likely be during meetings of great importance such as an interview or lunch with current or potential donors. These are not exactly the times you want to flounder with your fingerbowl!

The basics of dining are pretty standard territory for any etiquette book or magazine column. There are even thousands of videos available on YouTube covering this topic. Figuring out your salad fork from your dessert fork should not be a problem. The trick to this type of skill though is practice. Therefore, if possible, it might be worthwhile to look into local resources to actually put these skills to the test. Many local colleges hold workshops for students to help them build this type of business acumen. Additionally, there may be local etiquette experts willing to give a one-time lesson. Either way, learning how to flourish during more formalized dining events can give you an extra boost of confidence. That confidence can then allow you to focus on what is really important, the conversation, rather than your place setting.

Resurrecting the lost art of the thank-you note can help set you apart from the crowd. Sending these notes does not have to be relegated to some formal event or activity. Although it is always good practice to follow up something formal such as an interview with a thank you, many other small interactions can benefit from the gesture too. Nothing shows coworkers, mentors, or new connections your appreciation quite like a handwritten note. Some would argue that e-mail is now king when it comes to thank-you notes. And it's true that e-mail is convenient, fast, and can be shared more easily. However, the experience of receiving something tangible, written in real ink, with a tailored message, emphasizes the sentiment you are expressing. It highlights your willingness to go that extra step. It shows the receiver they were worth the additional time and attention it took you to send the note to them. Who wouldn't appreciate that? We all want to feel that what we contribute is important. Thank-you notes acknowledge our interdependence and convey that you are someone worldly enough to know it.

Lastly, remember to pay attention to your handshake and eye-contact behavior. Again, proper etiquette will be dictated by circumstance and even culture. However, these two behaviors send loud and clear nonverbal signals, often before we have even opened our mouths, which can instantly color someone's perception of us. Disagree? Think about it this way: would you buy a car from someone who looked everywhere but your eyes? My guess is probably not. Avoiding eye contact can be interpreted by others as a variety of qualities such as dishonesty, submission,

Top Five Networking Habits to Cultivate

- Develop good nonverbal cues.
- Cultivate your listening skills.
- Broaden your connections to span all areas and levels within the profession.
- Review your online presence regularly.
- Remember to be gracious; you never know where you might meet someone again.

Top Five Networking Habits to Avoid

- Talking without asking questions
- Oversharing personal information
- Scanning the room while actively engaged in conversations
- Drinking too much
- Only speaking to people you know

Action Items Recap

- Spend some time brushing up on the norms of social etiquette.
- Set small attainable networking goals—remember quality not quantity.

or discomfort, just to name a few. These are definitely not messages we want to convey while we're in the process of networking. If you're unsure what messages your handshake or eye contact are saying about you, ask a trusted friend or loved one to give you feedback. Once you know what impressions you are sending out, you can work on fine-tuning these cues to send the right message to whomever you're socializing with.

PARTING THOUGHTS

Networking is an integral part of succeeding in the library profession today. It has the power to both open and close doors of opportunity. Although not always a natural talent, learning how to do it right is an important tool for any powerhouse librarian.

In order to move forward and get things done right, we need more than just our own talent and experience. We need to know and connect with other people who can bring fresh perspectives, different thought processes, and resources that may not be part of our personal repertoire. In other words, we need a village. No matter where you are currently in your career, it is never too late to start networking. Start building your village today.

REFERENCES

Baumeister, Roy F., Ellen Bratslavsky, Catrin Finkenauer, and Kathleen D. Vohs. 2001. "Bad Is Stronger than Good." *Review of General Psychology* 5 (4): 323–70.

Still, Kaisa, Jukka Huhtamaki, and Martha G. Russell. 2015. "New Insights for Relational Capital." *Electronic Journal of Knowledge Management* 13 (1): 12–28.

5

Building Your Guest List
Identifying and Leveraging Valuable Stakeholders

How This Might Look in Practice:

- Host a library open house every semester to bring together current and future stakeholders.
- Research individual audiences and tailor marketing messages directly to them.
- During discussions focus conversations on where both agendas intersect.

So, we just finished discussing why and how to grow your social network. Making connections is a powerful tool in your personal arsenal and essential to any successful powerhouse librarian. However, it's not enough just knowing how to create allies within the profession. To successfully get things done, you also need to know when, where, and how to leverage those connections appropriately.

Every project, workplace, community, or environment inhabited by intelligent life has a set of stakeholders. This fact is an important one to recognize early if you plan to achieve anything in a reasonable time frame. According to *Merriam-Webster*, a stakeholder is "one who is involved in or affected by a course of action." Neglecting to acknowledge that a project's success, and your success, largely hinges upon outside relationships can stop a good idea cold. Although the media and society love to glorify being a diva (oftentimes with a capital *D*), this is one area where that outlook can have serious repercussions. True powerhouse librarians know that getting things done is

---

Important Tip

Before starting important conversations, make sure you check your ego at the door. Most successful relationships require give and take. Although strong-arming may get you what you want in the short term, it can cost you in the long run. Evaluate what you want before talks begin, so you'll be better prepared to compromise.

---

all about the collaborations—not the personal pursuit of glory. How do you know if you're navigating into diva territory? Take a minute and run through this quick library diva checklist. Ask yourself the following:

- Is what I'm doing about me or something greater?
- Do I view a team success as just as big a win as a solo success?
- Is it about me or we?
- Do I acknowledge others' expertise and strengths in making things happen, or do I focus on what I bring to the table?
- What do I do when someone disagrees or suggests an alternative? Do I listen and consider or shut them out?

Don't worry if you answered a little more "me" then "we" at this point. The above questions were more about getting you to recognize your personal bias before you start engaging people. It is okay to want recognition for a job well done. But it is also important to remember that stakeholders need to be recognized too.

To successfully engage with library stakeholders requires some preplanning. The following sections in this chapter will focus on defining, identifying, approaching, communicating, and evaluating stakeholder relationships.

DEFINING STAKEHOLDERS

Having a clear idea of what constitutes a stakeholder is an important first step in preparing for success. Basically, in the simplest of terms, a library stakeholder is someone who will be impacted by the actions you take. Students, faculty, community members, employees, research scientists, board members, and administrators can all be categories of stakeholders depending on your flavor of library. A stakeholder can appear above or below you in the library organizational chain. It could be a clear relationship from the beginning, or may need to be investigated more fully to identify all of the potential connections. Stakeholders could be at the individual level or encompass an entire group or organization.

It is important to remember that as the size of your project grows, so will the number of potential stakeholders. This concept is especially important during the early phase of planning and cannot be overstated for those who are just developing their powerhouse skills. Take your time and reflect on who should be at the table. Even seasoned project-management professionals can grapple with this task! In a study reviewing stakeholder management in mega construction projects, the authors note that "notwithstanding their professional knowledge or experience, the accuracy of assessment and judgment of project managers often decrease as the project grows in size and complexity" (Mok, Shen, and Yang 2015, p. 447). If this is an area that even the professionals need to be mindful of, take heed—so should you. Count your stakeholders early and often, because if you don't you could experience serious ramifications down the road.

IDENTIFYING STAKEHOLDERS

When it comes time to start identifying potential stakeholders, it can be helpful to take a few minutes and ask yourself the four questions of who, what, why, and how. By making yourself answer these simple (and sometimes surprisingly complex) questions before talking to various groups, you will begin to get a better picture of possible talking points and how to frame future conversations. This is an important step and one not to be missed. I repeat. This is an important step and one not to be missed! Different stakeholders will care about different things, so messages should be tailored accordingly. Below are some sample questions that might fall into the who, what, why, and how categories. Depending on the project or service you might ask the following:

Who

- Who will be impacted now or in the future?
- Who needs to be approached early versus once the project has traction?
- Whom do I need support or buy-in from versus those who just need to be aware?

What

- What is important to each stakeholder I need to approach?
- What information or education do I need to prepare before talking to people?
- What possible concern might surface for this group?
- What questions do I need answered from the various stakeholders?

Why

- Why is this project being undertaken, and what is the impact if it does/doesn't happen?
- Why is this stakeholder important to be considered?

How

- How might various stakeholder needs be similar or different?
- How can conflict be handled if need be?
- How could what I'm doing be viewed and possibly misinterpreted?

After taking time to answer these questions for your specific situation you should have a pretty good idea of who needs to be engaged and how you might approach them. From here you can start grouping your stakeholders.

Generally, for most kinds of library projects, you will have two types of stakeholders to consider: internal and external. Each group will have to be approached differently based on their respective status. Warning: when possible, true powerhouse librarians know you should start with your internal stakeholders first. Why, you might ask? If you do not have the proper buy-in from those groups meant to support your service, you cannot be successful. Without solid internal support, any challenge that

---

Important Tip

After your brainstorming session you will likely have a good idea of who needs to be included, as well as excluded. Make sure you spend some time thinking about why certain parties might not be the right stakeholders. This will help you feel prepared should you be asked by the powers that be at a later date.

surfaces may be used to justify delaying, understaffing, or flat out deny-ing your endeavor. Take the time to talk to people within your library first—especially those outside of your department! Internal stakeholders could include those in specific areas such as management, administration, operations, systems, public services, user experience, and web services. Or for those of you in management, they could include all employees (student, staff, professional, and librarians).

If the idea of employees as stakeholders is new to you, I might suggest starting to investigate the literature in this area. According to research conducted by the Boston College Center for Corporate Citizenship, "Employees are increasingly considered to be among the most important group of stakeholders" (Smith 2013). Upon reflection, this insight seems obvious. Employees are the lifeblood of any library. However, how often during discussion and planning is the immediate focus placed upon those we serve? Even if a project is patron geared, taking a moment to consider simple ways to recognize contributions to the project once it is underway can go a long way toward improving morale (and smoothing the way for people being more open and willing the next time you need support on an initiative). Long-term success is driven by sustainability. And that sustainability is achieved by the efforts of those colleagues who surround you—at all levels. Be sure to recognize that and act accordingly.

External stakeholders are equally as important to consider from the beginning. They will be the ones to ultimately consume your product (un-less the project is meant for internal use only) or the ones you will need to open doors for you. External library stakeholders could be anything from your users to other departments that you need to collaborate with and funders. Your flavor of stakeholder will really be dictated by your envi-ronment. It is important to recognize that these groups will likely be mo-tivated for different reasons than you are (or your internal stakeholders). Therefore, you will need to spend time getting to know them and finding a common language. Many good library projects get sidelined because the parties involved cannot effectively communicate with one another. Or worse still, energy and enthusiasm are squandered on something that users either don't understand or don't find valuable or necessary.

I've been working on a team for a grant-funded project for the past sev-eral months. We had some ideas about directions in which we thought we wanted to go in developing the end product: a mobile app for emergency responders. Early on, using contacts that had been made through conference attendance and a disaster symposium that had been held in the area, we reached out to members of the emergency response community to participate in a focus group and run our initial ideas by them, and of course to get their input and feedback. And it's a good thing we did! Thanks to the participants of that focus group we learned that our initial concepts were simply not heading in the right direction. Members of the group were very gracious in sharing how they thought our project and product could be improved and better meet their needs. We were able to go back to the drawing board and recraft our product because we brought in these stakeholders very early in the process. The app has since launched, initial feedback has been positive, and we are getting ideas for future enhancements. This process was a reminder of an old adage: know (or get to know) your audience. (GK)

As illustrated above, valuable time and energy can be saved by spending some time gathering feedback first. Although it may add time onto your timeline, engaging with stakeholders early can make sure you stay on the right track. It's well worth the effort to ensure a positive result at the finish line.

APPROACHING STAKEHOLDERS

Depending on your timeline and connections (aka the people who know people), it might be wise to spend a bit of time researching each prospective group. If the stakeholders you are working with are new to you, it is important to make a good first impression. I know what you're thinking—well, thanks for the tip Captain Obvious. However, I am always amazed at how unintentional or unaware people can be during this critical time period. Current research shows that we make up our minds about someone within the first seconds of meeting them (Wargo 2006). Think about it. In a fraction of a second you're lucky if you've been able to even make eye contact. By the time you have managed to crack a smile or open your mouth, your stakeholders have already unconsciously gauged whether or not you are someone they would consider working with or helping. Amazing, no? To make sure you start off on the right note, here are a few tips to keep in mind when striving to make a positive first impression:

Dress the part. How we dress says a lot about who we are. Take a moment to consider if you are sending the right impression. One of the best pieces of advice I ever received was to dress for your next job.

Body language. How you carry yourself says more about how you're feeling than the words you choose. Make sure to make eye contact and offer a firm handshake, even if you're feeling nervous. Note: Remember back to the last chapter. If you will be working with stakeholders of other cultural backgrounds, spend some time learning what is culturally appropriate and mind your body language accordingly. Different gestures can mean different things across cultures, so you will want to make sure you are aware of what might be construed as inappropriate.

Smile (and mean it). Humans are built to read those around them and look for signs of danger. Smiling puts people at ease—so long as it is genuine. Offering a smile upon greeting lets the person know you are there with positive intent.

Being intentional about how you want to be perceived is a proactive step in the engagement of your audience. You cannot control the ultimate outcome, but by being mindful about the power of first impressions, you have a better chance of starting the conversation out on a high note.

In addition to learning about the groups you will be working with, it is also important to know the main areas of potential impact for the different stakeholders. This is where our research skills can come in handy. Take time to recognize that what you might perceive to be as a small impact could in fact have larger implications for the group you are approaching. And the size of that impact could influence your stakeholder's willingness and ability to buy in. It's important to ask about any unknowns and stay open to the information being shared with you. Be prepared to take any new information you learn into account. Flexibility is a vital skill in working with library stakeholders. Agenda pushing in the face of new information is unlikely to win you any friends or cement the support you were hoping for.

Now there are many different factors that can influence how open each group you need to work with might be to your project or proposal. Possible pain points could be environmental politics, past experiences, pending changes, staffing, and budget. In researching stakeholder engagement, Stephanie Missonier and Sabrina Loufrani-Fedida note that "in order to identify stakeholders and understand their evolution throughout the project, practitioners have to observe not only human but also non-human actors that they produce or put into circulation and their associations and influences during the project." (2014, 1119). If available, taking time to understand the context of each group's situation before engaging can be enormously beneficial. It is amazing how effective taking someone to coffee can be to find out the best way to approach outside groups. Make sure to leverage, and further encourage, these kind of interactions by acknowledging and thanking those who provide you insight. It doesn't need to be anything grand. A simple phone call or thank you will do. Building allies before high-stakes meetings can help you feel more confident and can assist you in effectively communicating the value of your library proposal if need be. Having an external champion who "gets it" can help explain things in a different way, and foster postmeeting excitement.

Now that you have learned about each group, developed your talking points, and mindfully tried to make a good first impression, the important work begins. Taking time to listen during this first meeting is just as important as knowing what to convey. Good listening skills can help you make connections between shared goals and also give you information to identify potential future obstacles. Spending time actively listening to each group or person's "story" can also be a powerful trust builder, if approached in a genuine fashion. True powerhouse librarians know that we all want to be heard. Making sure stakeholders feel they are important contributors, by connecting back to what they've shared, rather than passive recipients will help people feel connected and empowered. Empowerment breeds engagement. And this is exactly what you will need to successfully get things done.

COMMUNICATING WITH STAKEHOLDERS

Now that you have taken the time to establish partnerships, setting your focus on keeping people informed and on the same page is needed. WARNING: If you want to be successful, and keep moving forward in a timely fashion, do not overlook this step. Now you might be saying to yourself, "I always know what's happening." If you are one of those lucky individuals who is always in the know, well, I say (1) good for you, and (2) your experience is probably not the case for the vast majority of people. Let me provide some context for you on why failing to establish good communication channels is a big deal. Communication failures can be the kiss of death to keeping people engaged and positive about your project. Bad communication can cause all kinds of mischief. Some of the most common hijinks include the following:

- Duplication of work
- Missed deadlines
- People working on "old" priorities
- Confusion on who is responsible for what
- Mixed messaging
- Underutilized services
- General frustration

The list goes on and on. Eventually even the most excited stakeholder will become weary, and the great energy you spent all that time cultivating will be redirected to greener pastures. Game over. Don't let this happen to you! The following are some proactive steps you can take to keep your communication flowing.

Take time to discuss and set expectations. Making sure that everyone is clear about their role is the foundation of ensuring your project stays on track. Stakeholders who are unclear of what job they have run the risk of duplicating work or neglecting core tasks. These knowledge gaps can cost your project big in terms of time and resources. Clearly articulating roles can not only make library stakeholders feel vested in your project but also keep you from having the "that's not my job" conversation down the road. The expectations talk should happen early and be revisited periodically. During the course of discussion, key elements should be reviewed such as action items, timelines, and any team norms you want to establish.

In addition to setting expectations, consider establishing a communication plan. Powerhouse librarians know that keeping everyone on the same page can be difficult but is necessary to developing a cohesive team. Determine what norms will work best for everyone. Can stakeholders expect a weekly e-mail to be kept in the know? Will groups be expected to proactively check a team SharePoint site? Whatever plan you determine, make sure to not only discuss it but also document it for everyone. This can be useful for two reasons. The first is that following up with an e-mail allows any miscommunications to surface quickly. The second reason is that by writing down the expectations, you can refer back to that communication and create accountability. Good communication plans may include

- frequency of updates;
- method of updates;
- who is responsible for communicating what and with whom; and
- norms for internal and external communications.

Plans can be as detailed as you like. However, remember that once the plan is developed (hopefully with some input), you will have created an expectation that you will need to follow. Make sure that any adjustments to the plan are shared to ensure you are meeting stakeholder expectations.

Finally, you may have to develop a few strategies to keep all parties informed. For example, in addition to holding in-person meetings, perhaps you could also provide written minutes. You can send out e-mail reminders and updates. However, maybe you could post them to a shared space as well. It may seem redundant, but having a backup mode of sharing information can save frustration down the road if someone feels left out of the loop. Overcommunicating is typically preferable to the alternative. By establishing an information backup plan you are then in a better position to shift the onus onto any grieved party. Plus, having a multipronged approach shows your stakeholders you are trying to be proactive and transparent—a huge trust builder for any group.

REFLECTION TIME

As with anything, taking time to reflect is an important part of improving for your next attempt at getting things done. Figuring out what went right and what went wrong will help improve your efficiency for next time. Take time to gather feedback from those library stakeholders you engaged in your project. Did they feel they were brought in at the right time? What worked for them? What didn't? Showing you want to improve their experience can strengthen your relationship and build your credibility for future collaborations.

Five Good Stakeholder Habits to Cultivate

- Identify and engage groups early.
- Learn to speak their language.
- Know what is important to each player.
- Listen.
- Establish norms to keep everyone on the same page.

Five Stakeholder Habits to Avoid

- Assuming your goals are the same as theirs
- Believing you have no stakeholders
- Approaching every group the same way
- Failing to recognize the power of first impressions
- Assuming

It can also be helpful to debrief on learning points for you. Sometimes there will be standout things to take note of. However, spend some time identifying other, more subtle experiences you should be mindful of next time. Working with stakeholders is all about getting to know people. Taking time to figure out what you can capitalize on or incorporate more quickly next time will help expedite the relationship-building process.

PARTING THOUGHTS

Engaging stakeholders will always be a constant for any project you plan to undertake. Whether we are developing something for consumption, improving a process, or changing a model, our actions rarely have implications only for ourselves. The way we choose to interact with the people around us directly impacts the ease of which we can get things done. Focusing on developing a strong collaborative outlook, mindful of inclusion, is something true powerhouse librarians strive to do.

Remember, stakeholders take the form of both internal and external audiences. Be willing to explore their similarities and differences. Leveraging each groups' strength can not only improve the present project but also set you up for successful collaborations in the future. This is also a great way to expand your resume, by building strong partnerships that can open doors to other opportunities you may never have imagined. So be bold, partner well, and reap great success.

Action Items Recap

- Spend time contemplating who, what, why, and how.
- Determine internal and external stakeholder groups.
- Establish best practices and a communication plan.

REFERENCES

Missonier, Stephanie, and Sabrina Loufrani-Fedida. 2014. "Stakeholder Analysis and Engagement in Projects: From Stakeholder Relational Perspective to Stakeholder Relational Ontology." *International Journal of Project Management* 32:1108–22.

Mok, Ka Yan, Geoffrey Qiping Shen, and Jing Yang. 2015. "Stakeholder Management Studies in Mega Construction Projects: A Review and Future Directions." *International Journal of Project Management* 33 (2): 446–57.

Smith, Katherine. 2013. "Positive Stakeholder Relationships Build Trust and Business Value." Boston College Center for Corporate Citizenship, August 7. http://corporatecitizenship.bc.edu/.

Wargo, Eric. 2006. "How Many Seconds to a First Impression?" *Observer*, July.

6

Walking the Beam
Creating Balance

How This Might Look in Practice:

- Develop an engagement or wellness program unique to your library's needs.
- Highlight "balance" wins of library staff members.
- Do a balance check when developing new library policies (as appropriate).

How to achieve a "balanced" life has been a hot topic of discussion for decades now. We hear it screamed through media headlines such as "how to have it all," "the work/family conundrum," or "finding inner harmony." Weekend conversations center around how to do all the things we've neglected to do all week. The topic has produced gurus, workshops, and so many self-help books you would be hard pressed to walk into a bookstore or library and not be able to find an assortment of titles to choose from. With so many people thinking and talking about the topic, one would think the solution would have been found by now. And yet, years after the conversation has started, we are still struggling to figure out how to fit it all in.

As the world becomes more complex, connected, and timeless (as in 24/7), the struggle to find some semblance of balance becomes a more urgent issue. Gone are the days of business being done Monday through Friday between the hours of 8:00 a.m. and 5:00 p.m. Our cultural expectations have shifted so radically over the last fifty years that a store being closed on holidays is now thought of as weird and inconvenient, rather than the norm. Finding balance in a world gone time-blind can sometimes feel like learning how to breathe water rather than air—impossible and unrealistic. Libraries are no exception to this pressure. Not only must we strive to find personal balance as individuals, but also our organizations must find strategies to do more with less, create meaningful services to very diverse audiences, and undergo cultural-driven metamorphosis while grappling with the question of what to keep and what to let go. And this is just one facet of modern life. Multiply the above by the realms of family, friends, learning, pleasure, wellness, community, and so forth, and it's no wonder finding balance (even imperfect balance) can feel more elusive than glimpsing a unicorn while finding the pot of gold at the end of a rainbow.

The truth is that balance takes constant work, self-awareness, and candor, none of which can be easy to maintain at times. However, true powerhouse librarians know that committing to finding balance is worth the sustained effort. Why? Without it, you will be unable to both get things done and maintain them over the long haul. And let's be perfectly honest, what is the point of building something brilliant only to run out of steam and watch it wither into nonexistence? Cultivating balance both within the library and within your life is the key to maintaining the fuel (aka your energy and resilience) to getting things done.

So what does it mean for you, a true powerhouse-librarian-in-training, to find balance? *Merriam-Webster* defines balance as "a state in which different things occur in equal or proper amounts or have an equal or proper amount of importance." I like this definition because it focuses on the key aspect of cultivating balance: the goal of equalizing the important parts of our life and work. We want to maintain a distributed focus so we avoid becoming so absorbed by one thing that everything else falls away. In essence, balance helps us to see the big picture so we can maintain a healthy approach to all of the nuanced facets that go into projects, relationships, services, and so forth. Without it, we may not be able to determine when we are going a little (or a lot) off course. Need an example? Reflect on the following:

> The library has decided to try to improve the collection's circulation. You spend hours designing a new marketing campaign to highlight the new ad-

ditions to your collection this quarter. You have identified the most exciting titles, solicited "recommended reads" by your coworkers, carefully crafted concise yet informative write-ups of each, and thoughtfully branded all of the materials with the library's logo. It has been a solid week's worth of work, and you are approaching the submission deadline. As you finally hit the send button to the various student, faculty, and staff distribution lists, you feel satisfaction wash over you. It's done. You've succeeded! Mission accomplished. Then the reference intern walks up to you with a printed copy of the flyer you just mass e-mailed. As she compliments the great choice of graphics, she wonders if you realized you misspelled the library's name in the heading.

We've all been there. This is a small but very common example of being too close to a project. Laser-like focus can be a big help in buckling down and completing a task. However, it can also create unintended blind spots that you might not realize are even happening. How often have you worked so long on something that you stop seeing the actual product as it is? Instead, you see it as you think it is—big difference. Being mindful of balance, in all aspects of what we do, can help us to avoid little hiccups as in the above scenario, as well as larger, more impactful disasters. In the following sections, we'll discuss balance in multiple areas of life, as well as how to spot when you're starting to stray from the balanced path.

FINDING THE BALANCE AT WORK

Let's be honest, working in libraries is a pretty sweet gig in comparison to a lot of other industries. We don't usually have the same pressures associated with typical "business" jobs. For instance, librarians aren't required to hit sales quotas, pitch products to clients, or deliver a new drug to market. We aren't operating on patients, defending someone at trial, or vying for a major multinational contract. However, we certainly can feel the pressure in others ways depending on what type of library you find yourself in. For instance, although we aren't the ones holding the scalpel or delivering the closing argument of a court case, we may be asked to find the information that informs that doctor's or lawyer's decision making, if you practice medical or legal librarianship. Although scientists are the ones in the trenches of developing new drugs to bring to market, a librarian could very well be responsible for identifying the competitive intelligence needed to ensure the drug succeeds, as well as the patentability of the final product. Suddenly the role of librarian/informationist/knowledge manager got a whole lot more interesting and potentially pressurized.

It is true that the work librarians do can have a measurable and important impact on the success of our organizations. The function of connecting the right parties with the right information at the optimal time is a significant part of what the library does. Our ability to be expedient and service oriented helps to ensure targets are hit, deadlines are made, and our patrons leave with exactly what they needed (or knowing it is on its way). I would argue that regardless of your role within the library world, the desire to help and be of service is a driving force behind what you do. In terms of balance, that desire can be a double-edged sword. On one hand it compels us to create, share, and collaborate on many different levels with many different users. Our ability to generate and then freely share what we made is an unparalleled hallmark of our profession. However, our commitment to being everything to everyone, whenever they might need us, can result in unfortunate side effects such as overcommitment (anyone else have problems saying no?), fatigue, chronic multitasking (even when we know we shouldn't), and eventual burnout. Suddenly, balance can seem like an impossible dream meant for others.

Finding balance at work can be difficult (especially if you are a solo operation), but it can be done. Below are some office-friendly behaviors you can implement to juggle task-related activities in a more harmonious way.

Prioritize your day. Looking at a giant laundry list of things to accomplish can be really overwhelming. Start the morning by getting rid of one to three easy-to-accomplish tasks right at the start. By knocking some low-hanging fruit off you list, you not only get a small win to begin the day but also eliminate the distraction of simple tasks that will nag at you while you try to finish other things. For longer-term prioritization, invest in a whiteboard and some dry-erase markers. This will allow you to color-code your list of ever-competing priorities to make sure attention is getting paid to the right areas. Plus, the board is easy to update should you need to juggle tasks unexpectedly. As a bonus, listing out your projects in this way can help coworkers and managers visualize just exactly what is on your plate before handing you a new project.

Call a timeout. It can be hard to establish boundaries with coworkers in general, let alone when you're feeling pressured. If the thought of turning someone away from your office freaks you out, try utilizing some signage. Placing a small sign on your door or cubical entrance that indicates when you're free (e.g., Available after 10:00 a.m.) can be an easy tool to limit unwanted interruptions.

Ignore your e-mail. Turning off your e-mail for brief periods of time can help you beat that pesky need to multitask. E-mail (like texting) has a bad habit of triggering our "I have to do it *now*" impulse. Eliminating that need, even for an hour, can offer essential uninterrupted concentration time, a key ingredient to getting things done. Granting yourself the ability to focus can move you from triage mode to feeling as if you're actually making progress. You will be amazed at how much you are able to tick off your list, and funny enough, those e-mails will still be there once you pull your messages back up.

Although small in their own right, implementing tricks such as these can help you build in breathing room into your day. Identifying and maintaining balance is a very personalized effort. The portrait of a balanced work experience will look different for everyone. Finding effective and efficient ways to cope is one area where the onus will definitely be on you. Since balance is one of those things we can't necessarily see, few folks are likely to notice when there is an imbalance until something negative happens. The next section is targeted specifically at those of us with supervision or management responsibilities.

So, you've finally made it to the boss's chair. You're now responsible for not only overseeing your personal to-do list but also making sure that work is being accomplished by your amazing team of dedicated direct reports. The balance stakes just got higher. What you might not have realized initially was that with these new leadership responsibilities, not only are you responsible for ensuring balance for yourself, but you also need to make it a priority for those people around and under you. Surprise! Welcome to library management.

Important Tip

As with so many things we've discussed, brainstorming with a buddy can help yield other creative solutions that can be tailored specifically for your environment.

Now you might be wondering why someone else's balance is all of a sudden your responsibility. We're all adults. Employees should be able to take care of themselves, no? My answer to you is, it depends on what type of leader you want to be. Ideally, because you're reading about becoming a powerhouse librarian, you want to strive to be the best. Exceptional leadership starts with the ability to empathize. People can't be creative, productive, standout librarians, assistants, or paraprofessionals if they are feeling overwhelmed, completely consumed, or frustrated with their jobs. When work gets to the point where you can no longer see the forest for the trees, you're starting to get into a productivity danger zone. And that my friend is bad for business.

As a manager, you have direct influence on what balance looks like for your team. As Valerie Morganson, Michael Litano, and Sadie O'Neill so eloquently state, "Managers play an essential role in facilitating subordinates' ability to balance their work and personal life roles" (2014, 226). How? Let's take a look at some of the things you as a manager are responsible for doing that influence your employees' experience:

- Distributing work projects
- Being an information conduit regarding organizational benefits, norms, policies, and so forth
- Establishing departmental expectations and norms around important topics such as communication and taking leave
- Setting deadlines, goals, and deliverables
- Determining working conditions regarding schedules, telecommuting, and so forth
- Giving performance appraisals

The list goes on and on. What you set as the standard and emulate as a leader directly and indirectly influences your workplace. We send clear messages

---

Important Tip

There is a ton of work currently being done around empathy and compassion in a number of different fields. For a broad perspective, check out literature from psychology, business, and medicine, amongst other fields. They can provide you with important insight into the benefit of empathy from multiple angles.

to those around us by our attitudes, actions, and behaviors whether we are aware of it or not.

Trying to emulate good balance yourself can give unspoken permission to those around you to put their needs on the list of tasks that need prioritization. When you strive for balance yourself, and share the experience with others, the importance of the pursuit can slowly work its way into the culture and become self-sustaining. This can lead to group accountability for member wellness. "A positive work-family culture encourages members of the organization to support one another in their work-family endeavors. In fact, research suggests that supportive workplace relationships mediate the relationship between work-family culture and work interference with family" (Morganson, Litano, and O'Neill 2014, 236). When leadership gives permission for employees to be human, we can weave that empathy into the colleague experience. It's easier to be balanced when you know nobody is judging you for it. Prioritizing balance as a leader can help short-circuit the competitive mind-set that sometimes develops within work units.

This can translate into positive tangible benefits in terms of productivity (e.g., number of books cataloged) and commitment (lower turnover and absenteeism). Both are good indicators of a library's organizational health and well-being. This can lead to benefits far beyond just making individuals happy (Rampton 2016). Satisfied employees can lead to a variety of impactful benefits including the following:

- Top-notch recruitment. Nothing sends a stronger message to candidates than the vibe emanating from the current culture and employees. Happy, healthy, productive employees can help attract and retain talent across the library.
- More creativity. Problems inevitably arise, no matter how much of a well-oiled machine your library might be. Promoting balance as a core value can help employees attack problems with a refreshed perspective and vigor. They will be more likely to identify better ways of doing things. Librarians or paraprofessionals who constantly feel too bogged down in "doing the work" are less likely to have the bandwidth to step back and try a new approach.
- Deeper commitment. Staff members are more likely to feel committed to you when they know you are committed to them. Libraries are

notorious for having hierarchies between librarians and, well, everyone else. Committing to and communicating balance for everyone
can help break down some of those barriers and strengthen relationships across levels.
- More fun. Humor, laughter, and enjoyment are all important elements
  for dynamic, responsive, creative libraries. Cultivating balance at the
  employee and leadership level can help everyone build a buffer to absorb challenges and negativity when they arise. This ability can help
  prevent a minor setback from developing into a full-blown meltdown.

On average, full-time work consumes nearly 25 percent of our available
time in a given week. Depending on location, accounting for commute
time could push that number up even more. That is huge given that theoretically almost one-third of our time is spent sleeping. The time we spend
working is no trivial component of modern-day life. Finding balance at
work should be a daily practice that we all commit to. Leaders have direct
influence over every aspect of a library's culture and mentality. Still not
convinced? Check out our powerhouse librarian case study:

I'm an extrovert, so for me I get charged spending time with friends and
family and being out and about. I try to say yes when people want to get
together or [when I receive] invitations to birthday parties. By promising
someone time, I feel I have a real reason to get away from the work. So
that helps me mentally. Have hobbies and make time for them. Do what
you need to for your health, both physical and mental. Therapist? Exercise
regime? Nutrition classes? Go for it. I do check my work e-mail at night. I
expect my librarians to do so but only to answer urgent student questions.
(We don't have a librarian on duty after 5:00 p.m., and our reference stats
prove we don't need one, but we do like to keep an eye on requests that
might come in.) But I do have a rule about vacation. Don't look at work e-
mail if you are truly on vacation. *Don't.* Just don't. If there is an emergency
a phone call is a better way to contact than an e-mail.

Work and life need to balance. I stress that with my employees, and I try
to emulate that for them. I only work late if I have a real deadline. I don't
e-mail them from home or on weekends unless it is urgent. I'm flexible
with people's schedules and my own. I think if you have an atmosphere of
respect for each other and a joint belief in your institution's mission, people
will work well together. (KT)

True powerhouse librarians know that cultivating a balance at every level is key to any library's long-term success. A library without balance may continue to plug along, but it's unlikely to ever truly get ahead and inspire.

FINDING YOUR PERSONAL BALANCE

Balance can be a complex thing to identify. Part of the challenge is because balance is so uniquely personal. What feels perfectly reasonable to one person may be completely out of whack for another. In addition, how we create balance can be changed and influenced by circumstances in our life. Internal and external circumstances may circumvent our best intentions even in the most mindful of us. In short, there are a lot of nuances to the balance equation, and we are never fully in control of all pieces.

If the idea of not being fully in control freaks you out, take heart. There are practical things you can do to influence the art of balance in your favor. But more on that later. Like our discussion on work, having an imbalance in the other "soft" areas of your life can create just as much havoc personally as in the work sphere. And unfortunately, just as work can hemorrhage into your personal life, so too can the opposite happen. Having too many personal obligations to balance can interfere with your ability to become a powerhouse librarian on the professional front. The need to balance pleasure, family, friends, school, community, faith, and health can spill over and come out in performance issues such as absenteeism, tardiness, constant mobile connection, difficulty concentrating, and so forth. Yes, that work-life balance can cut the other way too, my friend.

Most of the boundaries we have in life are gray and squishy at best. And for many of us they need to be. We often need to be flexible to deal with the changing landscape we are always trying to navigate. What we really need to be aware of when we talk about personal balance is when imbalance begins morphing into deficit. We see this happen most often when it comes to our health. When life gets stressful for most of us we usually feel that something has to come off the list. There are few things that we generally get to choose to do. We need to work to eat. Our family and friends provide us with stability and kinship. Oftentimes the things we sacrifice—for instance, sleep, working out, and meditation—are those self-care things that take a while for the consequences to surface. Unfortunately, when they do, the issues associated with our neglect—such as high blood pressure, depression, and weight gain—can have very negative consequences that can last long after our stressful period resolves.

So how can we strive to create balance when it may not be possible to do everything? Below are a few tips you can try to help pull you up by the bootstraps when you feel imbalance or deficit is getting the best of you:

Acceptance. Accept that you will never be able to be 100 percent balanced. Life just doesn't work that way. Instead, focus on making progress rather than being absolutely perfect. Cutting yourself some slack can help take the additional emotion out of the situation that often comes with our own judgmental self-talk.

Remember there is always tomorrow. If you fall down on being balanced today, you always have a chance to try again tomorrow.

Prioritize "me time" first—literally. Start your day off doing something for you. If you know the day ahead will be too full to work in time for healthy activities, do them right when you wake up. This could be exercising, meditating, reading, or even sleeping in for an extra fifteen minutes. Our bodies are pretty good at telling us what they need. Listen and do accordingly.

Set an intention. If you intend to make room for a balanced life, you will be more likely to find ways to accommodate everything you need to do. Knowing that you intend to get everything done can help you regain your feeling of control when life gets too out of control.

Give it a voice. All too often we're afraid to say when we're feeling unbalanced. We fear words such as *overwhelmed, depleted, raw, overcome,* or *inundated* because we're afraid if we say we feel this way others will equate it to weakness. However, others can't help us rebalance or rebuild if they don't know we're feeling an imbalance to begin with. People aren't mind readers. Use your voice to say what you need. Nobody else will do it for you.

A fully balanced life never looks exactly perfect. There will be times when you feel more balanced than others. Finding balance should not become a stressful activity. If you find that in trying to reconfigure things you're more stressed out than before, you are likely putting too much pressure on yourself to find a perfect solution. Accept this now: a perfect life does not exist. The goal is to strive for a harmony that is equal-ish in as many facets as possible. Let's be clear: this is not the same thing as settling. Settling would be surrendering to all the competing priorities we have out of a sense of defeat. Striving for an equal-ish resolution offers you the realization that you have a level of control while simultaneously accepting you can't control everything. In essence, a balanced outlook falls somewhere between the ideal and reality.

BALANCE AND THE CREATIVE

We talked in depth about creativity in chapter 3. In fact it is such an important topic to the future of librarianship that we are going to touch upon it again here. Creativity is the new currency of librarianship in a lot of ways. We utilize it to improve our services, strategize on how to do more with less, and advocate to those constituents who might not always clearly see the library connection. The ability to engage in creative problem solving and visioning is a powerhouse skill that is always in demand regardless of role, status, or job function.

One of the biggest impediments to creativity is imbalance. Part of the reason for this can be explained by the resulting stress of imbalance. When we feel we are always playing catch-up on tasks, goals, and commitments, the future can suddenly become a crushing rather than a motivating force. The stress of the present begins to bleed into the possibility of the future, replacing optimism with distress. We begin seeing events as either impossible or a burden limiting our desire to engage. These mental frameworks undermine the foundational elements creativity needs to blossom—an open mind, energy, and willingness to participate.

In addition to stress, imbalance also causes us to lose focus. When we feel pulled in a million different directions, nothing receives our full attention. Our mode of operation morphs into a frantic dance of triage, procrastination, and autopilot. We cling to routine because we know the likely outcome without having to sacrifice the few precious brain cells we have left to deal with the inevitable fires that always arise, and because, silently, we know these are the times when we will be called upon to deal with an irate patron, budget cut, or broken website. At these points focus is only for emergencies, not creative flights of fancy.

However, creativity can be an important part of generating balance. Our creative brains can help us identify new ways to develop and sustain balance when our routines go awry. Flipping our mental filters (otherwise known as our outlook) is an important part of dealing with stress and life uncertainty. Creativity can help us find a way to marry what seems like a conglomerate of disparate pieces into a cohesive flow of life. It can help us identify and map out similarities that can help to improve our efficiency in switching gears. If we only need to make small mental leaps rather than huge detours, the sense of pressure imbalance creates starts to dissipate. Creativity can serve as a temporary buffer to the negative side effects of imbalance.

The hard part of the equation is cultivating creativity when we're stuck in the chaos cycle. Most of us aren't likely to stop in the middle of teaching a class or updating our OPAC to contemplate creative solutions when we're feeling the heat. We need a trigger to step back and gain some perspective. Below are some simple ideas for how you can work in creative problem solving on the fly.

Find a theme. Take five minutes and look at your giant to-do list to see if there are any tasks/events that naturally partner or complement one another. Try to batch things together to create an organized flow. For example, if you have a class to present in a different building, have paperwork to deliver to HR, and are supposed to pick up a gift copy of Dr. Smith's new book for the collection, your day can feel a bit crazy. The theme to the above tasks is that they all take you out of the office. Instead of doing errands in the morning and teaching in the afternoon, organize your time to do them in one fell swoop. You will minimize your back and forth, freeing up time to do other, equally important tasks.

Flexible chunking. Use your creative brain to look for things that may be able to split into pieces. Chunking may be not ideal, but it can help you find time when your calendar is filled to the max. For example, if you have a day where you have several committee meetings all over campus and are likely to miss your workout, see if you can build workout elements into your transit time. Walk or bike to your meetings instead of taking the shuttle. Do one set of different exercises before or after a meeting (e.g., stair climb, standing push-ups, and holding a plank). By thinking creatively you can utilize that "wasted" time in a new beneficial way.

Believe and bend. Know that you have the ability to find a better way to accomplish everything you need to. Believe you are flexible and creative enough to find a new approach. Be willing to modify how you are going about doing things rather than forcing a flow that isn't working. Balance requires adjustments, so don't be afraid to adjust strategies as often as needed.

The most exciting thing about engaging your creativity to find balance is that you can continually tailor ideas to match your needs of the moment. Creativity offers you the opportunity to reframe a problem into a workable solution. We will never have enough time to accomplish everything we want to do. However, creativity gives us a chance to blend, flip, reframe, or mash-up what we find most important into a picture we feel is livable and ideally beneficial in the long run. We all want to be happy, and enlisting our most creative self to help make that happen ensures a positive outcome for both the present and the future.

HOW TO SPOT WHEN YOU'RE OUT OF BALANCE

One of the challenges about balance is that it is not something you can tangibly monitor. We feel pressure to clean our house because we can physically see the evidence of what happens when we don't: dishes, dust balls, and piles of laundry. The concrete evidence of our decision not to clean accumulates, accosting our senses (visual, touch, and smell) until we are motivated to address the problem. Balance is trickier to address. It sneaks up on you, surfacing in unexpected and unpleasant ways. We may not think about it until someone brings it to our attention. Think performance appraisal or our annual physical exam. Or we may realize it suddenly as we're lying in bed unable to face the day or showing up an hour late to our anniversary dinner for the second year in a row. Not very happy pictures at all.

There are usually warning signs along the way. They may be subtle or indirect. There may be a crop of seemingly unrelated but important events that happen, signaling we are headed for a balance disaster. True powerhouse librarians have learned how to both detect and correct these early warning signs. The following are some early warning signs you can monitor to make sure you stay on a balanced track.

Motivation changes. Sometimes we just don't feel like mustering the energy to attack that pile of teaching paperwork, leering back at us and waiting to be filed on our desk. Occasionally loss of motivation is totally normal. We get fatigued from a bad night's sleep, start coming down with a cold, or spend six hours straight designing a complicated spreadsheet to determine next year's purchases. Our demands are complicated and varied, and sometimes we just don't have the energy to face the next task waiting to be tackled. However, a persistent drop in motivation could be a signal that things are starting to go awry. If you find you have several days in a row where you just can't seem to find your mojo, it's time to step back and evaluate what's happening.

Sleep changes. Rest is an important facet of maintaining our health and well-being. However, changes to our sleeping patterns (either more or less sleep) can signal we're feeling the pressure somewhere. If you are experiencing more than occasional disruptions to your sleep, it's time to step back and recalibrate.

Behavioral changes. We all have ups and downs. When multiple hiccups surface in different parts of our life, sometimes it can be hard to maintain that silver-lining attitude. But if you've suddenly morphed from a glass-half-full kinda gal to Eeyore, you might be sliding into imbalance. Not so sure this is happening to you? Start listening for the kinds of descriptors you're using in conversation. Our word choices can be good

---

Top Five Habits to Cultivate

- Reflect often on your internal state, outlook, and choices.
- Leverage your creative mind to accomplish your to-do list.
- Accept that a balanced life does not necessarily equal a perfect life.
- Think in terms of small improvements rather than radical changes.
- Ask for help when needed.

Top Five Habits to Avoid

- Waiting for other people or circumstances to restore balance
- Thinking balance looks and feels the same for everyone
- Developing a mind-set that you must be connected to your technology at all times
- Accepting imbalance as a permanent state
- Ignoring or dismissing early warning signs as they pop up

Important Tip

Although the above flags can indicate balance issues, they can also be indicators of other important mental and physical health problems. If you have questions or concerns never hesitate reaching out to your health-care provider.

indicators for our mind-set. Language can be an insightful tip-off to how you and the people around you may be feeling.

Fun factor. Remember the last time you did something you enjoyed? If the answer is no, a while ago, or fun—what's that? you're headed to the balance danger zone. Stop and unplug immediately.

Outlook changes. How we view incidents, events, and our commitments can provide good insight into our balance state. If activities you once looked forward to suddenly feel more stressful than enjoyable, you may need to survey what has changed. It could be that you truly no longer enjoy attending lunch-hour walking club. But it could also mean that you need to talk to your boss about reprioritizing your projects. Either way, changes such as this warrant consideration of the situation.

PARTING THOUGHTS

As with anything worth pursuing, balance can be a tricky pony to wrangle. You will think you have a handle on it, only to hit a roadblock, forcing you to rethink your perfect strategy. Balance is a moving target even at the best of times.

The positive thing to remember is that we are all striving for the same thing at varying levels. Having a balanced life is something that can be worked toward whether you are a library assistant, systems administrator, or director. True powerhouse librarians recognize the benefits balance can bring at both a personal and an organizational level.

Once balance is achieved not only are we able to perform better but also we have the opportunity to tap into our best creative selves. The ability to connect with our creativity, foresight, and entrepreneurial spirit are lifelines in this ever-changing profession. Librarianship of tomorrow is forged on the vision of today. To have that guiding clarity we must be

Action Items Recap

- Implement tiny adjustments to help bring focus to the day.
- Reflect often to identify any red flags of imbalance.
- Remember our attitudes and actions can filter into the world around us. If you're promoting balance, make sure you are reflecting that in your actions!

able to see as many facets as possible. Balance can bring the centeredness needed to inform such monumental choices.

In the end balance helps us bring our best selves to the table. And in the end we're better librarians for it.

REFERENCES

Morganson, Valerie J., Michael L. Litano, and Sadie K. O'Neill. 2014. "Promoting Work-Family Balance through Positive Psychology: A Practical Review of the Literature." *Psychologist-Manager Journal* 17 (4): 221–44.

Rampton, John. 2016. "How Work Life Balance Can Keep Your Employees Happy and Your Business Healthy." Inc., February 29. Accessed August 25, 2016. http://www.inc.com/.

7

Realizing It Takes a Village
Developing a Team Mentality

How This Might Look in Practice:

- Implement an internal team mascot to help foster departmental identity.
- Establish regular channels to cross-train at all levels.

By this point on our journey to becoming complete powerhouse librarians, it should be pretty apparent that focusing beyond yourself is a key takeaway of this book. Although it's important to own all the awesome you bring to the metaphorical library table, it is arguably more important to understand just how that awesome fits in and bolsters the awesome of others. No matter how talented, smart, or funny you are, success does not happen in a vacuum. We need other people. It's nearly impossible to become the best librarian in your organization without the talent and skills of those around you to help pave the way. Where most people spend time focusing on their agenda (and we all have them—they are called goals, desires, etc.), your job is to think about how your natural strengths and abilities can benefit others. True powerhouse librarians recognize and focus on how to help others grow along with themselves. They focus on what brings us together rather than what sets us apart.

Developing a team mentality may surface more naturally in some than others. And that shouldn't really be surprising. Considering the world from a global level, modern American culture is currently all about the individual. Marketing campaigns are tailored to tap into our egos. They often focus on our uniqueness and desire to stand out from the crowd. Conforming is the enemy. We are compelled to attend (or send our children to) elite level schools, because that branding can set us/them apart from peers. Local media outlets focus heavily on our carved-out pockets, rarely covering national or foreign events beyond the surface. Where people used to know the neighbor all the way down the hall, we often no longer know the name of the person in the apartment next to us. For better or worse, it seems our world has exploded and shrunk all at the same time.

Talking about teams probably feels both natural and a bit foreign in the context of personal growth and success. The way libraries are organized automatically shuffles us into unofficial teams called departments. We're organizationally a part of tech services or systems. We identify as research or instruction people. But beyond that, we more often than not focus on our specific niche within that larger department (or team). We are specialized into an island unto ourselves. How often do we spend time connecting how our role impacts or dovetails into other areas at the back or front of the house?

A number of things can impact whether or not a specific team succeeds or fails at delivering what was asked of them. Sometimes the breakdown happens because of complete external circumstances, such as funding, re-organizations, and changing deadlines. However, sometimes it's the ability of the library team to come together that stands in the way. Too many people look through the "I, me, they" lens and are unable (or—gulp—unwilling) to shift into we. Or perhaps there are too many people trying to lead, or completely polarized stylistic approaches. It happens. We've all witnessed or been a part of this type of slow, painful stall. Below is a case study highlighting just such a scenario.

> I'm currently on a strategic planning team. Since we are a small group, all staff members are on the team. However, we do have subteams working on each of eight strategic goals. So far we have not been successful since our first meeting, which was led by outside facilitators. Why not? Some of it is work style. There are definitely people who want to make sure every *t* is crossed and *i* is dotted before you even think of actually accomplishing the work. There are others who want to jump in the deep end right at the beginning [but who] now know how deep the pool is. Those varying personalities, the small size of our staff, and the fact that each subteam has

> **Important Tip**
>
> If this topic is of particular interest to you, consider checking out Patrick Lencioni's book *The Five Dysfunctions of a Team: A Leadership Fable* or Kerry Patterson and Joseph Grenny's *Crucial Conversations: Tools for Talking When the Stakes Are High.*

a different leader but is also on three or four other teams has led to much doing of nothing. We can't always have outsiders come in and get us to work together. What to do? Maybe we are stretching too thin. For such a small team maybe we should limit the number of goals to something more manageable? Maybe there are people who should not have leader positions or maybe they have the wrong leader positions? How do we get back on track? Not sure yet. (KT)

The line between whether teams succeed or fail is whisper thin. This chapter is designed to help you, dear reader, identify what you personally bring to the table, create well-formed library teams, and think at a broader level to move those teams ahead.

KNOW YOUR ROLE

Now that we've spent the first part of this chapter talking about needing to shift from an I to a we focus, we're going to take some time to talk and think about—wait for it—ourselves. Fitting, right? This is actually an important step, because without self-knowledge, we can't effectively identify and leverage what we bring to a group. Instead, our tendency is to often gravitate toward what we want to be doing (desire driven) versus what we excel at doing (talent driven). If we're lucky, our talents and desires overlap, making this a nonissue. However, sometimes we need a reality check of our skill level.

Getting a handle on our array of talents and skills can be a tricky business. Oftentimes we don't truly know all of the skills and talents we excel at because we utilize them on autopilot. A problem or task arises in the library, and we just tackle it without deep contemplation. Given the myriad of things we need to accomplish every day, it makes sense that we wouldn't spend gross amounts of time trying to identify what skill we're implementing at the moment. It's impractical, and potentially inhibitive, to getting things done. At the same time it's also possible to have a skill blind spot. This is more likely to occur when we let our ego selves into the driver's seat.

To most effectively identify where your talents can best be put to use in your library, I propose taking time to create a personal SWOT analysis. For those of you who may not know, a SWOT analysis stands for strengths, weaknesses, opportunities, and threats. SWOTs are commonly used tools in the business world when assessing a product or entity's viability. It helps a team's members to take inventory of what they are currently doing well, as well as things they need to consider that can throw a wrench into things. A personal SWOT can be an essential part of figuring out just where you might have the most impact or the types of obstacles you might stumble on. Ideally, if done right, a personal SWOT targeted on both you and the task at hand can help paint a picture of what types of team members you might need to bring into the fold.

Although this can theoretically be done mentally, writing down your inventory can help spark important insights to take into consideration. At the end of this chapter, I have included a precreated template you can use to begin your personal analysis. For many of us the inclination is to just start doing a brain dump. However, I recommend taking some time to think through the following.

Strengths

Although this may be tempting to think about only in the context of work—don't. Situations and environments can influence what talents we implement on a regular basis. We use the skills we're called upon to use and that may not always be reflective of the pool of talent we possess. Take some time to think about the following:

- What do I spend a good amount of my waking time doing?
- What aspects of the activities I undertake do I enjoy most?
- How do I generally approach a problem I need to tackle?
- When I need to get things done, what strategies do I employ?
- If I asked library colleagues about my strengths/talents, what would they likely say?

The list could go on and on. The goal is to think about our strengths broadly, as various projects (or components of the project) may call for different things at any one time.

Weaknesses

Remember to be objective here. It can be challenging to step back and critically appraise where we need to grow without getting all self-loathing. Our weaknesses are often easier to self-identify than our strengths! But we need to remember that our growth areas may already be places where other library team members excel. Consider the following:

- What types of activities or projects do I really grapple with?
- What early warning signs do I start to exhibit when I'm really struggling with something?
- Are there any themes I can identify for activities I struggle with or dislike that can help pinpoint any weaknesses?

There is no expectation that you are going to magically be great at everything you undertake. And more importantly, if you can't identify areas to improve, then you might be at risk for a personal blind spot. Make sure you take the time to openly and honestly evaluate all parts of your SWOT inventory. This is for you after all!

Opportunities

This is likely where the context of the project will begin to surface in connection with your strengths and weaknesses sections. The vision here should be forward looking and taking into account both the present and the future. Some questions to consider may be as follows:

- Are there new skills I can implement and grow based on this opportunity?
- What avenues might be opened up?
- How can I use or do x in a new way?

Your opportunities are likely be shaped based off of your current outlook. So since opportunities might require a bit of creative thinking, this section

> **Important Tip**
>
> Getting feedback about our strengths and weaknesses from outside observers can be a real help to get a 360-degree view. Enlist the help of a colleague you know and value to give you the dish on where you're great and where you can grow. And remember, feedback is an invaluable tool. Take it at face value.

would be a great time to utilize some of those creative tactics discussed in chapter 3 (walking meetings anyone?).

Threats

It is important to identify how you define "threat." These do not necessarily need to be things that wreak damage or cause harm. Threats could also be thought of in terms of competition or inefficiencies. Questions to ponder might include the following:

- Is there a duplication of skill sets?
- What inefficiencies in process might you be working with?
- What is happening in your environmental landscape?
- How might your personal landscape come into play?

After completing your personal SWOT analysis you will have a better understanding of both what you bring to the table as well as areas you need to enlist extra help. By identifying both assets and hurdles at the beginning, you can effectively identify what skills and attributes need to be added to the team to make your task a success. True powerhouse librarians know that by gaining a clear picture of the current situation, they will be in a better spot to plan and act appropriately.

THE BENEFIT OF DIVERSE PERSPECTIVES

We can't talk about developing a team mentality without talking about diversity. According to *Merriam Webster*, at its most elemental level diversity means "the quality or state of having many different forms, types, ideas, etc." By definition, libraries should be, and generally are, leaders in this arena. We purposely build our collections to be comprehensive and worldly. We champion the freedom of expression and the accessibility of information to anyone who seeks it. At our very core, libraries are the safe havens for all perspectives to come together (whether in person or in print) to share, learn, and grow. The idea of diversity is built into our very DNA.

Although we deal in the theory of diversity on a variety of levels, libraries are not immune to building programs or staffing models that are more homogeneous than intended. Even given the varied communities we serve, and the various skill sets required to do our jobs, we still need to actively monitor and build teams that reflect the diverse perspectives we need to be considering from our user bases. The truth is, diversity is a key ingredient to successfully getting things done. In order for any library team to truly excel, a variety of experiences need to inform the conversation. Why? Being able to think from different perspectives means we are better able to anticipate the path ahead. We will be less likely to be stymied by unforeseen circumstances because our frame of reference will be broader, more informed, and possibly more accurate.

There has been a flurry of recent articles talking about cognitive bias and its impact on our decision making in the world and the workplace. Our unconscious biases, generally shaped by our societal standards and experiences, leak their way into our work spaces and end up reflecting themselves in issues such as pay equity and leadership (Nishiura Mackenzie 2016; Olson 2015). The unspoken attitudes that pervade our world sometimes show up surprisingly unnoticed but in glaringly obvious fashion. For example, think of the general lack of women and minorities in recognizable American CEO positions. We know this trend persists despite the volume of these different groups in the workforce. Why?

As humans, our natural habit is to seek out the familiar. The familiar is safe, and our primitive brains are wired to find that security. However, we may unintentionally be missing opportunities for greatness by misguidedly trying to build a harmonious culture based on similarities. "Members of a homogenous group rest somewhat assured that they will agree with one another; that they will understand one another's perspectives and beliefs; [and] that they will be able to easily come to a consensus" (Caleb 2014). In essence, it's a lot easier to drink the library Kool-Aid when everyone else does too.

We crave that easy comfort of recognition. But it may be that erroneous way of thinking that is actually undermining our success. As one author nicely sums up this pitfall, "Unfortunately, too many would-be leaders seeking flexible, adaptive and resilient teams actually produce ordinary performance by diligently hiring employees who too closely resemble themselves and others on the team" (DeGrosky 2009, 10). In our effort to create comfort we may overlook the diversity that can help us thrive. In essence, in an effort to find the "right fit," we mistakenly believe that similarities will improve our likelihood of achievement by improving speed and efficiency, and that by creating a group full of like-minded individuals, we will ensure consistent, high-quality, innovative work.

The truth is, that simply isn't so. Paul Caleb offers up a great example of this in his article related to the scientific literature (a topic near and dear to many a librarian's heart). He references a study, conducted by Harvard affiliates Richard Freeman and Wei Huang, that looks at the impact diversity has on scientific research papers. Their study found that teams who were more diverse were actually cited more often than teams that were not (Caleb 2014; Freeman and Huang 2014). Who knew? But if you truly think about it, that fact shouldn't really be too shocking.

Not surprisingly, diversity allows us to tap into a collective wisdom far beyond what our own internal frameworks are capable of. When we have more experiences at our disposal we are better able to make connections in a new and innovative way. We gain the ability to see beyond what we currently know, because we have a larger pool of information to work from. Plus, we have team members who are able to provide a counterperspective that can help surface roadblocks we didn't even know existed (or challenge established assumptions). Diverse teams can be one of our best assets for avoiding inertia, a problem that can be the kiss of death for any library.

It's important to remember that when we talk about diversity, it can take on a variety of forms. Diversity goes far beyond the standard checklist we are all likely familiar with. It surfaces in our work experiences and life experiences, our interests, and our approaches. The topic of diversity is particularly important when you start to think in terms of that SWOT analysis at a departmental or library level. Too much of a certain mind-set or strength can be just as detrimental as too little. Where the hope is often that similarity will be binding and create cohesion, it can also backfire and create competition, blind spots, groupthink, and impasse. It is important to remember that as teammates (or perhaps team leaders) we have direct power to help bring diversity to the forefront. Check out the case below highlighting the beauty diversity can bring to helping a team accomplish its goals:

> I was recently on a planning team for a state conference for medical librarians. The conference went very smoothly due to the fact that each member of the planning team had a clear role, and each person took responsibility for their part of the planning and organization process. Also, team members each used their strengths to the advantage of the entire group. For example, one person was a good "idea person" and came up with a creative theme for the conference. Another gal had a flair for graphic design and was able to design a conference flyer and also put content up on the association's website. And yet another managed the financial and business aspects. The woman leading the team scheduled regular meetings where we checked in and gave updates about our progress. If there was something left undone or unanswered we would establish a deadline by which it would be accomplished. In other words, we helped keep each other accountable in a positive way, working toward a common goal. Lastly, I have found that often people just want to be asked to contribute, and not everyone will be the first to step up or step in. But, if they are asked directly to do a concrete task or to take on a clear project, they will often say yes and are pleased to be able to contribute. It helps to remember to ask people who aren't always the first to volunteer. That way, you get a good representation of team members from a variety of backgrounds. (GK)

True powerhouse librarians understand that to cultivate a diverse team sometimes means looking beyond your normal "go-to" people. This is a particularly important step for those of us in the library profession—one that is heavily weighted toward a more introverted constituency (Williamson and Lounsbury 2016). Just because some people don't automatically leap on an opportunity doesn't necessarily mean they aren't interested. They may need time to mentally process and assess before speaking up. Being mindful of that need can be key to making sure you are building a well-balanced and representative library team.

Thriving libraries come from a mixture of the right talents, a clear mission, and a breadth of experience to inform the process. Creating diverse teams should be a top priority for any powerhouse librarian.

> **Important Tip**
>
> Encouraging everyone to participate in the conversation is an important safeguard against groupthink. Remember, just as some people not immediately raising their hands to volunteer doesn't necessarily indicate disinterest in participating, silence doesn't always convey agreement or consensus. Following up with quieter colleagues individually after meetings can be a good practice to ensure all voices are considered in the decision-making process.

REFLECTING THE RIGHT ATTITUDE

So much of our attitude and outlook is conveyed to the world through the language we use and the nonverbal cues we signal. The words we choose, the tone they are delivered in, and the gestures we make (or don't make for that matter) all paint a picture of what we really think about something. Somehow it becomes hard to believe people are "fine" when they are standing in front of you stiffened, with their arms crossed and their eyes trained on the floor. It's important to realize that you can't just say you have a team mentality and (cue the magical fairy sounds) it suddenly becomes so. You have to truly work on creating that mental outlook, and it starts with the attitude you bring to the table.

For this section, we're going to begin with an activity. Find a partner, and complete the following exercise. If you are the one completing the activity, *do not* look at the partner role:

You

To start, take a moment and think about the last team project you were on. Now, imagine how you would describe that project: the group, the task, the results, and the final outcome. Go ahead and describe it to your partner.

Partner

I said *don't* look! Okay, partner, your job is to write down how often the person describing the project uses words such as *I* or *me* versus how often the person uses *we* or *us*. Keep track so you know, but refrain from labeling the *I*'s and *we*'s until the person has finished describing the experience. Once the task is complete share the results.

How did you do? Did the *me versus we* get the best of you? If you didn't do so well, take heart. Now that your tendency is on your radar, you are likely to do much better thinking about your future word choices. The point of this activity is not to make anyone feel bad. We're all human, and it's normal to gravitate toward thinking and talking about your role, outlook, and experience within a group. But it's important to remember that little things such as talking in singular can send a distinct message to listeners whether you mean it to or not. And if your default lands more toward the *I* outlook, it can have a big impact on team cohesion and morale—especially if you are in leadership.

Consciously trying to use inclusive language can help you not only start to cultivate a strong group dynamic but also begin to see interrelated connections within your team and library. When you shift your thinking of the library from a mash-up of parts to a single, living entity, the reality of the library as a complete ship relying on every position to keep it afloat becomes clear. As you begin to understand and appreciate the value of what each person brings to the table, you also enhance your standing and contribution as a recognized team player.

Although using inclusive language is an important component of a team mentality, true powerhouse librarians know that the team spirit can't stop there. In addition to being able to recognize the connectedness within your organization, you also need to be willing to recognize your library teammates for their contributions—big or small. There are few things more motivating than knowing what we contribute is acknowledged and appreciated. Peer-to-peer recognition (coupled with recognition from management) can help solidify team member commitment, a key ingredient to high-functioning teams. Being a valued member of the team strengthens our desire to not only succeed but help those around us succeed as well. Some small ways to recognize colleagues could be as follows:

- Acknowledging their contributions to your work on a designated team space such as a wiki or team bulletin board
- Writing quick thank-you sticky notes and leaving it at their desks
- Making sure any compliments you hear about them make their way to both your colleague and their supervisor
- Incorporating positive feedback about the team experience during project debriefs

Top Five Habits to Cultivate a Team Mentality

- Own group wins and group failures.
- Give positive and productive feedback.
- Share openly and graciously.
- Mentor when you can.
- Look for the larger impact beyond today.

Top Five Habits to Destroy a Team Mentality

- Minimizing others' contributions
- Withholding information
- Monopolizing team time and resources
- Failing to see your impact on others
- Expecting help and support without being willing to give in return

Positivity can be infectious. If someone does something to make your job easier, or helping the project you're working on stay on track, don't stay silent. Acknowledge the person's contribution with gratitude, and watch the team mentality take hold.

PARTING THOUGHTS

Developing a team mentality takes discipline and dedication. It is a skill that continually needs to be honed, and to truly become a standout team player takes time and practice. However, the benefits extend far beyond the tangible rewards often sought for a job well done.

Approaching your work with a team mentality can improve your desirability and organizational street cred within the library. Who doesn't want to work with someone who knows where they excel, works to understand what others contribute, tries to bring different parties to the table, and celebrates others' success as well as their own? The answer is, no one!

True powerhouse librarians know that when they help others succeed, the door to getting things done opens wider and wider. It may not happen immediately, but it will happen. Working to become an exceptional team member can help you stand out from the crowd, as well as keep the crowd moving when necessary. The time and energy you dedicate to helping everyone in the library succeed will help cultivate your own success now and in the future. It's time to focus on the team win!

Action Items Recap

- Perform personal and group SWOT analysis.
- Monitor your language.
- Build teams with an eye toward diversity.
- Personally acknowledge other team members' contributions.

Table 7.1. Your Personal Powerhouse Librarian SWOT

Goal:

Strengths	Weaknesses
Opportunities	Threats

Insights:

1. _____
2. _____
3. _____
4. _____
5. _____

Action Plan:

REFERENCES

Caleb, Paul. 2014. "How Diversity Works." *Scientific American*, October. http://www.scientificamerican.com/.

DeGrosky, Mike. 2009. "High Performance Requires Diverse Team." *Wildfire*, November/December, 10–11.

Freeman, Richard B., and Wei Huang. 2014. "Strength in Diversity." *Nature* 513 (7518): 305.

Nishiura Mackenzie, Lori. 2016. "Equal Pay Day: A Call for Stretch Leadership." Linkedin Pulse, April 11. Accessed April 15, 2016. https://www.linkedin.com/.

Olson, Elizabeth G. 2015. "How Corporate America Is Tackling Unconscious Bias." *Fortune*, January 15. Accessed April 16, 2016. http://fortune.com/.

Williamson, Jeanine M., and John W. Lounsbury. 2016. "Distinctive 16 PF Personality Traits of Librarians." *Journal of Library Administration* 56 (2): 124–43.

8

Being Smart and Flexible
Know When to Lead and When to Follow

How This Might Look in Practice:

- Know every staff member's name, and use it regularly.
- Honor the leader in everyone by recognizing acts of leadership at both the professional and the librarian level.

In the last chapter we discussed the value of teamwork and membership. In this chapter we will explore developing ourselves into the next wave of library leadership—whether or not you find yourself in the manager's chair.

Leadership or the ability to lead is a critical skill in libraries today. Many of us are feeling the palpable potential (or pressure; choose your preferred *p*) of what lies around the next corner. Our world has transformed in so many unanticipated ways. We have digital natives, rising health-care costs, changing political landscapes, increasing expectations of personalization (education, medicine, technology, etc.), privacy questions, and a myriad of other meaty topics ranging from burgeoning to full-blown disruption. In their article "Taking Library Leadership Personally," Heather Davis and Peter Macauley aptly summarize this reality by calling out old models of leadership thinking. They state, "It is no longer appropriate to be led by industrial era thinking with its roots in the 19th century and depicted by

heroic leadership and command and control practices. We advocate leading ourselves and our organisations in ways that incorporate the volatility,
uncertainty, complexity and ambiguity that now marks our lives" (2011,
41). As the world converges, librarianship finds itself at a tipping point;
and the type of leaders we choose to be will have an unprecedented impact
on how successful we are in morphing into our next incarnation. Choose
wisely, and we may have an opportunity to phoenix our way into being a
recognized and valued partner at the center of our organizations. Choose
poorly, and we could quite possibly lose what soft footing we have while
relegating ourselves into a cultural purgatory. The stakes are high and we
need to play to win.

In order to flourish into our best selves, true powerhouse librarians
know when to unleash their leadership skill set and when to fall in line.
They know that being a leader does not always mean having to be the
one "in charge" and that sometimes being a trusted member of the team
can bring greater rewards in the future if you have the right stakeholders
at the table. True leadership is not about ego, recognition, or personal ac-
complishment. It is about removing obstacles for those around you and
sharing in both the successes and failures as a partner, a champion, and a
teammate. As a leader, we must think no longer in terms of *I* but instead
in terms of *we*. Our focus must shift from the individual to the whole. We
must see the connections others don't. It is a tall task but one that offers
immeasurable benefit when done well. And lucky for you, dear reader, the
rest of this chapter is designed to help you succeed.

LEADERSHIP SKILLS EXPOSED

If you asked a hundred people what they thought made a great leader, the
words they use to describe that greatness would probably all be different.
But almost certainly key themes would emerge to highlight the traits or
skills required for success. The difference between good leadership and
bad leadership can often be felt and reflected in a library's culture. It
shows up in the language we choose to describe our experiences, projects,
or environments. Librarian or professional staff body language, tone, and
word choice all reflect to a certain degree what is going on at the layers
above them. For instance, think about the following scenario:

Your library has moved under a new umbrella of the organization. As part of this reorganization, library leadership initially reassures staff that there will be no position losses. However, there may be changes in responsibilities or reporting structures as the details are ironed out. The reorganization takes months. Leadership stays quiet during the changes, assuming staff will interpret no news as good news.

From your experience, what generally happens in this kind of situation? That's right; people talk. They may not talk directly to leadership, but they certainly talk to one another. And often instead of the silence being interpreted as "good," we fill the silence with our perceptions, fears, and so forth. Leadership's good-intentioned attempt to tell the story when there is one is thwarted by human nature. In the absence of information we fill in our own narrative. Communication fails.

The above example is a common scenario that happens every day in the workplace. Something is happening. Everyone is aware of it. But only a few key individuals have a part of or the whole picture. Communication is one of the top responsibilities that a leader has. People expect that being in leadership (at any level) gives you a plum seat to be "in the know" (whether this is actually true or not). Therefore the nuances of how we communicate (such as how, when, and where) are essential things to take personal note of. Because you are now in a position of "power" (and this is true for whether you're a big P or a little p), how you choose to treat the flow of information will be a big factor in how the people you're leading view you. It's important to understand that as a leader, we might be communicating without actually physically saying anything. For those who follow us, our body language, actions, decision making (style and actual choices), tone and demeanor, and so on, all send clear or unclear messages about what is happening in the world around us. Where we perceive silence as a clear signal that "nothing is happening," others may

---

Important Tip

Since communication is so vital to being a good leader, it is essential to spend time developing a strategy and style that works for you. If your library or organization offers educational support, definitely explore what courses they may have available. This is one area where you can never have enough training or practice.

interpret that action as secretive or a power play. Understanding the power communication has in a library is critical to the success of both you and your organization.

Given that communication is key, it pays to spend some time reflecting on how you tend to communicate and what (mis)perceptions you may be unintentionally sending out. Take a few moments and think about the following:

- What method(s) do I use most often to communicate with peers, direct reports, the boss, and higher ups?
- What types of information am I often communicating? Does my default method match the type of content being delivered?
- How often do I observe how my message is being received?
- When was the last time I got or solicited feedback on how I could communicate more effectively?
- Do I know how the people around me prefer to be communicated with?
- What messages may I inadvertently be sending out based on how I'm communicating?
- How often do I follow up and clarify when I think there may have been miscommunication?

One of the biggest mistakes reflection can help us avoid is mismatching our method of delivery with the message needing to be delivered. This is a particularly important step if you find that your preferred or default method of communicating is e-mail. Due to the flat environment of e-mail, it is *very* easy for messages to get misinterpreted. While this is a pretty normal occurrence, miscommunications from leadership can have negative consequences at a variety of levels across the library. Bad e-mail communication at the leadership level can often result in duplication of work efforts, budget mistakes, employee confusion, and so forth. If you find yourself in a leadership role, I strongly recommend you actively cultivate good e-mail etiquette and awareness, even if it means that e-mails take ten minutes to write rather than one. Remember your words carry weight, and people's priorities will be shaped by your directives, so it is imperative that your messaging is clear, is consistent, and invites others to clarify if necessary.

In addition to communication, great library leaders recognize that their staff is their biggest asset and empower them accordingly. As resources

Important Tip

Be mindful when using e-mail to deliver news that could carry an emotional charge. Determine if e-mail is really the best method for the type of news or message you are about to deliver. Utilizing e-mail should not be a substitute to avoid personal communication.

shrink, it is the creativity and ingenuity of those at the front line who find solutions and alternative pathways forward. Leaders who focus on cultivating autonomy and authority in everyone, beyond those with formal leadership roles, build a culture of ownership that drives high performance (Hendricks 2014). People are invested, and investment leads to better outcomes. There is a reason that this idea is a key principle recognized by frameworks such as Lean. In talking about various definitions of leadership, Davis and Macauley make the very astute observation that leadership in the "knowledge era" "is deeply tied to the sustainable use of our creative energies" (2011, 42). Modern life pulls us in a million different directions. Those things that we are most invested in are likely to get our prime energy and attention. Part of leadership is understanding that your job is not just to make sure "work" gets done but also to create an environment where every person feels he or she has something important to contribute and has the tools to do so accordingly.

So how do you know if you're creating a library that empowers its employees to be creative and to have authority and autonomy? Start by taking a look at your current environment. As you think about the situation, take some time to assess the following:

- Where do ideas, projects, and solutions come from?
- How often is feedback encouraged (and acted on) at all levels?
- Who gets included in the decision-making process?
- Are decision-making processes clear and consistent?
- When input is solicited, are people made aware of how that input will be used?

Starting to get a clearer picture? If you feel this issue is a gray zone for you, start by talking to your employees. That can happen in a variety of ways: think surveys, focus groups, and one-on-one meetings. Getting actual feedback is imperative here, because making an educated guess in this situation can create a real leadership blind spot. It's too easy to fall into that "no news is good news" trap that I mentioned earlier. One key thing to remember here though is, once you start asking questions, make sure you are prepared to do some work based off of what you find out. Nothing can damage staff morale faster than feeling they were asked to give feedback only to have it disregarded. True powerhouse librarians realize the bold move is not in asking the question but in taking the answers and making changes because of them.

So what happens if you asked the question and the responses were less than stellar? It's time to take action on what you can. Empowering library employees can take a number of different forms. Sometimes the issue and answer is simple (e.g., a change in process). Sometimes it's a bit more complex (e.g., effecting a culture change). The important thing is to commit to making a difference in an authentic way and communicating the why and how along the way. Some examples might be as follows:

- Clarifying processes to be more transparent
- Implementing group learning activities to enhance professional development
- Clearly articulating expectations around problem solving and decision making
- Inviting different stakeholders to leadership meetings if the topic is appropriate
- Making sure leadership shares in both team wins and team losses
- Acknowledging individual and team roles within the library

It's important to remember that no leader is ever an island. Staff is the lifeblood of any library. Great leaders recognize and honor that routinely.

Aside from communication, and empowering staff, the last thing truly great leaders do is inspire trust. It can be almost impossible to follow someone if you don't trust that person. And you can't be a leader, let alone a great one, if nobody is willing to follow you. What does it mean to be trusted? *Merriam-Webster* defines trust as "the belief that someone or something is reliable, good, honest, effective, etc." Based on this definition, essentially trust boils down to a set of behaviors or qualities that are observable to other parties over a period of time. Inspiring trust does not mean your followers expect you to be perfect. It doesn't require that you win every argument or that your decisions never go bad. Inspiring trust requires you to conduct yourself in a way that people believe you are concerned with both their well-being and the library's.

Given the fragile nature of trust, it's important to identify how and why it often gets broken. Knowing common barriers to trust at the leadership level can help you avoid falling victim to these pitfalls. As you think about your leadership journey, it's important to recognize that trust typically gets eroded by a pattern of behaviors rather than a single incident (caveat warning: depending on what the incident is). People generally recognize that mistakes happen to everyone. The trouble starts happening when the mistake or negative behavior becomes the mode of operation rather than a genuine misstep. Examples of behaviors that can undermine our credibility, and ultimately our trustworthiness, include the following:

Transparency. This complaint can happen in a variety of fashions. Most often transparency is cited as an issue around decision making and communication. The process isn't clear to everyone besides the person making the decision, so the staff ends up feeling as if decisions are made on a whim or some unwritten criteria they aren't privy to. If something such as a leader's decision-making process appears opaque or murky, it automatically triggers a feeling of "what are they hiding." It is almost impossible to trust someone if you feel the person is continually masking something.

Moving targets (also commonly referred to as mixed messages). We see this happen in politics all the time. A candidate starts off in one position and then slowly changes course, volleying between multiple positions depending on whom they are talking to. Don't get me wrong; there are legitimate reasons for changing a position on things. Sometimes new information comes to light, circumstances change, or a better, more cost-effective solution presents itself. It happens. But constantly oscillating between paths can make people feel you're playing sides or the vision is unclear. Neither scenario is good for trust building.

We? We who? Language can betray our underlying attitudes. Leaders that constantly forget to share credit can quickly isolate their followers and hurt productivity. Nobody wants to feel they are working to

---

Important Tip

Don't be afraid of looking through the business section of your local library or bookstore. Although libraries are not businesses, there are certain key principles that can help propel our organizations into their next incarnation.

---

make someone else look good without benefit to themselves. Leaders who are quick to accept team wins, but distance themselves from losses, can quickly undermine their credibility amongst staff and make their best performers look elsewhere.

Mea culpa. We all make mistakes. It's inevitable. But a leader who continually shifts blame to other factors, or worse, to team members, quickly generates a reputation—and not of the good kind. Nobody likes to admit failure. But being unwilling to say you made a mistake or that you're sorry as a leader is the ultimate dismissal of humility—a key component of good leadership. Being unable or unwilling to share in the blame is a clear signal to others that leadership can't be trusted.

Creating and maintaining trust is a much easier task than having to rebuild a broken bond. Neither battle is particularly easy, but building trusting relationships from the onset is vital to leadership success. Taking time to form good habits at the beginning of your leadership journey can help you both begin and end on a positive career note.

LEADERSHIP STYLES

In addition to cultivating certain qualities, becoming a leader is all about finding and cultivating an authentic style. Now there are any number of leadership models out there to choose from, for instance, servant, traditional, situational, and militaristic. You name it, and there is likely some type of leadership model available to suit every type of personality. It's important to recognize that styles are something that can be shaped and reshaped over the course of a career. Where something like our personality is pretty static, our style can be analyzed, refined, and molded to match a particular situation, environment, or organization (Murray 2009).

One of the most common pitfalls in leadership is to apply the same kind of leadership to every situation, regardless of what the circumstances might call for. Not sure what I mean? Picture this.

A high-powered American CEO is used to dealing with staff in an authoritarian manner. At work, the expectation is that directives will be delivered and carried out without question in the exact manner that is dictated. Very little input is gathered in the decision-making process, because as the leader, at the end of the day responsibility rests with the CEO. People are expected to understand and work within their station (according to hierarchy). At home, the CEO uses that exact same authoritarian approach (without change).

In today's day and age, what is the likelihood of this scenario having a happy ending? Where a hard-charging, take-no-prisoners, "I'm not going to listen to anyone" approach might work (arguably) in the business world, that same style or approach is probably going to go over less well in the context of a family unit. Now this example is a bit extreme, but it helps to illustrate the importance that context can play when selecting a leadership style. Applying the wrong approach, or approaching everything in a singular fashion, can take a serious toll on a leader's ability to influence and credibility.

In the How-To leadership series written for the *Wall Street Journal*, Alan Murray, author of the *Wall Street Journal Guide to Management*, discusses different aspects of developing one's style. In referencing the various styles developed by Daniel Goleman, Murray makes the observation that "the most effective leaders can move among these [Goleman's] styles [visionary, coaching, affiliative, democratic, pacesetting, and commanding], adopting the one that meets the needs of the moment" (Murray 2009). His insight touches on the need for a leader to have the ability to cultivate awareness—something that every true powerhouse librarian knows how to do. Throughout this book, I have talked about the need to take time to reflect and become self-aware. And this is still an instrumental step for a lot of different reasons. We need to be able to recognize what is driving us.

But as a leader, it is essential to realize that your awareness ability has to move beyond just yourself. In her article chronicling the evolution of leadership theories, Marci Martin ends her piece thinking about what is required of leaders today and advocates for this grander awareness. She

Important Tip

Because leadership frameworks are so varied, it doesn't make sense to cover them all here. What is applicable for a public library may be very different than what is needed in a law firm. Investigate and observe what styles are most applicable to your discipline or setting.

notes that for leaders, "recognizing your dominant leadership style is a good place to start in understanding what kind of leader you are. Knowing about other leadership styles, and using them when necessary, is the next step in your leadership evolution" (Martin 2015).

In more practical terms, think of it this way. A handyman doesn't only carry around a hammer expecting it will work for every job. It won't do him much good fixing a light bulb or repairing a tear in the carpet. Instead, he brings along an entire toolbox to apply the right tool to the right job. He takes time to match his tool to what he has to accomplish. The same is true for styles. True powerhouse librarians recognize that different situations will call for different things from them. There is no "one size fits all" approach when it comes to leadership (at least there shouldn't be).

It is important to reiterate the old adage that style and substance go hand in hand. Knowing and understanding leadership styles is not a substitute for developing the qualities that make leaders great. You still have to spend time developing the baseline qualities necessary for getting people to follow you. And speaking of following, that's exactly what we're going to talk about in this next section.

FOLLOW THE LEADER

I know it seems a bit silly to say it, but I'll say it anyway, you cannot be a leader without followers. It just can't happen. Now you might be thinking, well, duh. But I bring this up because occasionally there are people who want to be in (or could end up in) leadership roles who few people really want to follow. Now to be fair, there are a number of reasons this happens, far too many to discuss here. But we're talking about the notion of "following" in this chapter because of the instrumental role good followers have in our success. As one insightful librarian states, "Yes, leaders are important, but leaders and followers have a near symbiotic relationship" (Sullivan 2011, p. 14). Oh, how true that is.

It's important for both leaders and followers to recognize the power that followers have in their own right. In the article "Complementing Traditional Leadership: The Value of Followership," that power is highlighted. In calling out the follower skill set, the author states, "Long-time reference librarians, catalogers, and others outside the ranks of more traditional leadership positions bestow on their departments a depth of experience and dedication to excellence that is needed in a stable, thriving, and successful operation" (Currie 2014, p. 15). For leaders it is a good reminder that those who follow us are driven beyond our agenda. They have perspectives, opinions, and skill sets that can enhance the vision we are intent on creating. For followers, sometimes the daily grind can make us forget that we have the autonomy and authority to make an impact, even if "leader" isn't attached to our title. The value each role brings is influential to the overall project or organization at a much deeper level than we often realize.

Followership has started to gain a growing (albeit slow) interest in the management literature and, in my opinion, for good reason. Followers are the folks who get things done in our organizations. Where leadership might be responsible for charting the course and setting the vision, those who fall into the follower role are the ones to help those ideas materialize. It's advantageous from the leadership perspective then to help librarians and staff members realize their own contributions. As Jane Currie (2014, p. 16) notes, "Effective followers seek connections and use them to motivate their work, even aspects of it that might otherwise be perceived as mundane." Highlighting the contributions of effective followers can help honor the positive things they bring to our organizations, while reinforcing with staff that it doesn't necessarily take a formal title to make a difference. This is a very important point in our profession, since many in librarianship find themselves leading from the middle, sometimes even in senior leadership roles.

The truth is leadership is very fluid, and even leaders have to be followers sometimes. This is not to say that a leader needs to abdicate complete authority. But by stepping back and trusting a follower to be autonomous or take a guided lead on a project, you are a part of what can be a very empowering thing for everyone. Following, on occasion, can help you see things from the other side. It can expand our perspectives and help us experience what those we lead experience every day. Having that kind of firsthand knowledge at your disposal can be immensely beneficial to your leadership framework. This kind of personalized experience can help us approach situations with better listening, more empathy, and a deeper sense of compassion. These are all qualities great leaders bring to the table.

For those who have been in leadership a long time, stepping back into a follower role, even temporarily, may seem like a bold move. Check out below for a real-world example of how a leader/follower dynamic can look:

> I tend to lean toward taking the lead in situations, mostly because I am an action- and outcomes-oriented person. If I see that there is something that needs to take place or to change, I will often be the one to initiate at least a conversation about it to see where things stand and to help determine next steps. One example from recent experience is that I was on a planning committee for a national meeting, and I was cochair of a subcommittee. It turns out that my subcommittee cochair was in a time of transition at work as his library was being remodeled, so he was not as available to help organize things. The fact that I was aware of this helped empower me to take the primary lead on getting subcommittee members assigned and activated. When my cochair was able to "come up for air," he asked what he could do to help, and I was able to give him some assignments that really helped see our process through. Once the subcommittee members were established with their assignments, I was able to step back and let them work with a lot of autonomy and creativity. So, in essence, leading involves knowing the status of your team members and their availability and ability to contribute, setting clear direction and goals, and then trusting in your team members to accomplish their tasks. The leadership role is really one of setting the vision and direction, and then facilitating the work, allowing others to contribute using their individual strengths. (GK)

Here are a few more practical steps you can take to try and flex your follower muscles:

Start with a sure thing. Identify something straightforward in your library that needs to be done with a high probability of success. By selecting a project you feel confident about from the get-go, you are likely to feel more comfortable putting someone else in the driver's seat.

Recognize the power. Being willing to take a step back every now and again can have a positive impact on both you and your followers. Why? It shows you are flexible. Always needing to be in control can inadvertently send messages to those around us about how we might view them or feel about ourselves—regardless of whether it's true or not. Being willing to take a step back and be a part of the team, rather than always leading the charge, can demonstrate not only confidence in yourself but also trust in those around you.

Realize it is temporary. In reality your participation as a follower is likely to be a short-term thing. Projects have starts and finishes. Unless it is a huge undertaking (which in all likelihood would take it out of the running for delegation) the time commitment is likely to be low. Say one or two sixty-minute meetings a week or a month? In the grand scheme of things, having sixty minutes where you are not the one leading the charge is minuscule—and very, very doable.

Reflect on your followership. Remember you are likely following someone, somewhere already. We all answer to a boss. Reflecting on what you bring to the table as a follower can help reinforce the contributions we make outside of our leadership role.

Realizing that great leadership requires the ability to know when to lead and when to follow is key to becoming the kind of leader someone else wants to emulate. Honoring the role we all play, and being willing to step back every now and again, is a skill every powerhouse librarian works to cultivate. It can be hard at times to tame the inner ego and let someone else take up the reins. But your library, and you, will ultimately be better for it.

NONAUTHORITY AUTHORITY

Let's be honest; we can't talk about leadership without talking about authority. Authority, as defined by *Merriam-Webster*, is "the power to give orders or make decisions." Essentially, authority gives us the permission and power to decide the who, what, where, when, why, and how of a given situation or environment. Authority is what makes things happen, and without it, getting done what's needed can be a challenge. The trouble with authority is that for many of us in Libraryland, either we are not given direct authority or the authority we are given does not have the power behind it that other leaders are able to exert. So what are we to do?

True powerhouse librarians know that it is not the authority piece that is truly important to success. Yes, having ultimate authority over a decision is helpful. But the ability to influence, to get people to buy in, is what really drives decisions. And what's more, the ability to influence is luckily available to anyone, regardless of designated authority.

Unfortunately, the talent to influence is not something that everyone is inherently born with. Some people are naturally better at it than others. However, you can work on growing your ability and sphere of influence, and this can in turn can help in those situations where our authority is not inherent. Influence in libraries is not so much about making people see your point of view. In fact, if people feel that you are forcing your point of view onto them, you are likely to stop the conversations cold. Instead, it is about understanding what we do, being able to translate that into something meaningful for the other person, and sharing that story in a way that is impactful to them. Influencing truly needs to be delivered from the perspective of your target audience. Other important factors come into play in terms of timing, delivery, and relevancy that good influencers are always aware of.

Learning how to influence well is a skill that takes time to develop. Luckily, the ability to influence is a topic of interest not just to libraries, so there are plenty of learning opportunities available to those who are interested. Many of these opportunities can be found in marketing, business, psychology, or even library workshops and tutorials. To get started though, below are a few tips to keep in mind as you're thinking about how to influence your institutional or project decision makers.

> *Take time to listen.* People want to know and feel as if what they have to say is important. They want to know that you understand their perspective. It is very difficult to identify people's motivations or values if you don't stop to ask and listen. Finding out this kind of information is more easily done in a relaxed, neutral setting. People don't want to feel they are being pumped for information; so it is important to take a genuine interest in what they are sharing with you. Once you have a better idea of what is important to them in relation to the decision at hand, you will be in a much better position to connect their needs with yours.

Keep calm. It can be hard to stay calm when it feels as if things that impact you are out of your control. However, losing your temper can have a detrimental effect on getting people to understand your point of view. Letting your emotions get the best of you shifts the focus away from what you are saying to how you are behaving. Messages and intent easily get lost in a sea of emotion. In order to be able to influence effectively, you must be able to regulate yourself, especially when things are not going your way. Asking clarifying questions, pausing before you speak, acknowledging your feelings in a positive way, and giving others the benefit of the doubt can help keep conversations on track and your ability to influence intact.

Revisit. Sometimes the present moment just isn't the right time. Learning how to time your approach can help increase your ability to influence. If your decision maker is currently in crisis mode about something else, a drop-in meeting to ask about funding or starting a new service is probably not going to get the response you were hoping for. If things seem off, even if you have a scheduled meeting, asking someone for a time that works for him or her to revisit your discussion can help keep communication lines open. Since influence is so closely tied to how and when we communicate something, making sure timing is right is essential.

Navigating the authority chain, especially when you don't have any, can certainly be a tricky situation. Although no guarantee of success, learning how to influence effectively can be a key tool in your leadership toolkit. True powerhouse librarians know that although having authority is great, you can still make things work to your advantage with the right application of interpersonal skills. Assigned authority comes and goes, but influential ability can serve you well forever.

DEVELOPMENT

Growing into a great leader doesn't happen overnight. It takes years of learning—from your experience (good and bad), the experience of others, and the world around us. If leadership is truly a path you feel you want to take, figuring out a leadership growth plan is definitely worth your time.

As we talked about in the chapter on lifelong learning, the profession is constantly changing, and so we must too.

Developing a leadership growth plan does not necessarily mean charting your course to the top, although that may certainly be a piece of your overall career development. It means taking the time to identify what you need to learn and how you can go about doing it. Your individualized growth strategy can include as many or as few of the recommended pieces below as you choose. The value and applicability of most of these components depend on where you are currently at and where you want to go. Important elements to consider when thinking about your leadership growth may include the following:

- Mentors: both within librarianship and other industries
- Personal awareness: your strengths, weaknesses, goals, and motivations
- Assessment mechanisms: opportunities for feedback and evaluation
- Trainings: what is new or valuable to where you are going
- Experience: where you need to grow
- Style: where your mind-set and comfort zone are located
- Professional activity: when and how are you participating

Development is something we all need and should be an ongoing process. That doesn't change once you find yourself in a leadership role.

Top Five Leadership Habits to Cultivate

- Routinely recognize people within your library for the contributions they make—regardless of whether they report directly to you.
- Resist the desire to micromanage; delegate projects appropriately and then trust people to get them done.
- Set expectations.
- Communicate early and often—even if you have no new information.
- Ask what people need from you and honor it.

Top Five Leadership Habits to Avoid

- Assuming people know what you want or expect from them
- Believing you never have to apologize because you're in charge
- Shifting blame to members of your team
- Not knowing your people or understanding how processes work
- Thinking you (and the rest of leadership) always know best

Having a plan to proactively grow as a leader can help prioritize the learning process amongst your new responsibilities. It can also signal to those above and below you your commitment to being the best leader you can be. And honestly, who doesn't want to work for a truly great leader?

PARTING THOUGHTS

Leadership is one of the most interesting and complicated paths in librarianship. Sometimes we plan for it. Sometimes we just happen to find ourselves falling into the ranks. Regardless of how you get there though, true powerhouse librarians know becoming an exceptional leader takes time and a deep personal commitment to yourself and those around you.

Whether brand new to the profession or an old veteran joining the leadership ranks, the jump to leadership can be trying, complicated, growth inducing, and awe inspiring, sometimes all at once. It can leave you feeling heartbroken. It can leave you feeling gratified. There will never be a shortage of things to do or people who need you. The demands on you will be great.

But the rewards can also be so deeply satisfying, particularly when seeing the impact you can have on those around you, and the profession as a whole.

Times are changing. The need for great leadership has never been more pressing in our profession. We are at a tipping point, and those who lead today will decide the fate of those who join our ranks tomorrow. It's a brave new world with our destiny yet to be realized. Visionaries, creators, adventurers, and builders are all being called to realize this path. Powerhouse librarians must rise. Will you heed the call?

Action Items Recap
- Define a leadership growth strategy.
- Start identifying leaders you admire and the qualities that set them apart.
- Investigate leadership development opportunities available through organizations such as AAHSL, ACRL, and ALA.

REFERENCES

Currie, Jane P. 2014. "Complementing Traditional Leadership: The Value of Followership." *Reference and User Services Quarterly* 54 (2). https://journals .ala.org/.

Davis, Heather, and Peter Macauley. 2011. "Taking Library Leadership Personally." *Australian Library Journal* 60 (1): 41–53.

Hendricks, Drew. 2014. "6 Ways to Empower Your Employees with Transformational Leadership." *Forbes*, January 27. Accessed August 27, 2016. http:// www.forbes.com/.

Martin, Marci. 2015. "What Kind of Leader Are You? Traits, Skills and Styles." *Business News Daily*, July 21. Accessed March 25, 2016. http://www.business newsdaily.com/.

Murray, Alan. 2009. "How-to Guide: Leadership Styles." *Wall Street Journal*, April 9. Accessed March 25, 2016. http://guides.wsj.com/.

Sullivan, Doreen. 2011. "Leader or Follower: What If You're Not the Chosen One?" *InCite* 32 (4): 14.

9

Reenvisioning Ourselves
Focusing on Building Skill Sets Not Job Titles

How This Might Look in Practice:

- Build in a section around skill building as part of the library's strategic plan.
- Create skill-building workshops that cover both current and future needs.

As with anything, change is the only constant that the library profession can rely on. Over time, our focus has naturally shifted from creating and maintaining print collections to collecting and curating electronic materials. For many our spaces no longer contain books but are epicenters for collaborative learning shared with writing centers, career counseling, and cafés. We now have titles such as informationist, customer service manager, cybrarian, and knowledge manager. Our services and spaces are available 24/7, and patrons can check out the latest and greatest technology with a swipe of their library card. We have moved from hallowed gatekeepers of information to passionate advocates of access for all. In short, our landscape has changed considerably from our early roles and spaces.

Despite all of this morphing, it never fails to shock how often the phrase "that's not my job" is uttered in the library. Now, before you choose to skip this chapter right here, let me acknowledge that sometimes this is a valid response. It is not our place to physically escort disruptive patrons off the premises, or direct the food-delivery guy to the unauthorized pizza party in the upstairs student study room. We should not be babysitters, or diagnosing a patron's unusual-looking rash. However, more times than not, this type of reaction is not in response to a possible threat, policy violation, or lack of a medical degree. Librarians fall back on "that's not my job" in response to a myriad of service or organizational change–related requests. From personal experience, it is usually echoed by the phrase "I didn't go to library school for this." Now this topic is not being brought up to throw any shade at our library colleagues. More so, it's to draw attention to the fact that for a profession that prides itself on our customer service ethic, some of us sure spend a significant amount of time saying no. The question becomes why?

In her article "All Change: The Workplace Culture Challenge," Shaida Dorabjee discusses the culture of information professionals. As we've discussed in previous chapters, culture is highly influential in a variety of spheres. According to research done by the Special Libraries Association and the *Financial Times* in 2013, the future of librarianship will require professionals to be multiskilled, outward looking, and willing to stretch beyond their comfort zone (Lord 2014). Dorabjee (2015) advocates that there is a need to change our professional mind-set to be more open— open to experimentation, risk, failure, and change; you get the gist. However, she observes that "it is these softer issues concerning 'the way we do things around here' that have proved challenging at times, but which are essential to address in order to demonstrate good information management" (Dorabjee 2015, p. 42). The bottom line is, the plague of "that's not my job" is something that needs to be acknowledged and addressed head on. And it's up to the true powerhouse librarians among us to do it. Change is always around the corner. Let's find a path that allows us to meet the challenge on our terms.

ADDRESSING OUR PROFESSIONAL IDENTITY

Librarians spend *a lot* of time lamenting the perception of our profession. Whether fair or not, in popular culture we have been stereotyped as any of the following if you're a woman: as spinsteresque or the clichéd secret vixen. Both scenarios almost always require the female librarian to own a pair of dark-rimmed glasses. Male librarians typically get the honor of being stereotyped as either weak or bumbling. No matter what type of library the librarian works in, everything is always classified using Dewey. And magically, somehow every library looks as if it belongs in Hogwarts. Reality? I think not.

Part of the challenge for the library profession is that few people actually understand what it is that we do. There are likely a myriad of reasons for why this is the case. However, I see this particular issue as part education and part branding. In his article on library branding, Carl Grant notes that often companies cannot accurately see what their actual business is (Grant 2015). That is, they define themselves too narrowly (think format versus function). In talking about libraries he states, "Listening and reading about the profession of librarianship in our own time, you get a deep, gnawing feeling in the pit of your stomach that you've seen this scenario play out before. All too often, you'll find parallels between the examples just mentioned and what we're seeing professional librarians doing in shaping the perceptions of our users about librarianship. The problem is: Librarians' continued belief and acceptance of books as their brand" (Grant 2015, p. 100). We know that the conversation has shifted from library as institution to library as place over the last ten to fifteen years. Just look at the number of articles published in the library literature discussing space (Shill and Tonner 2003; Somerville and Brown-Sica 2011). Yet how often in our marketing and messaging are we focused on our collections? We spend our precious "face time" wanting people to know how much "stuff" we have. We list the number of journals we subscribe to, how many books we own, and how many computers we have. This focus on "stuff" leaves out the important message about what libraries are at their core: connectors and conduits to creation. Our brand is discovery, and the librarian is there to facilitate that journey.

Few librarians would argue our role as teacher, facilitator, and champions of access. But finding a word to encompass all of the things we do from a service standpoint is challenging. Opinions vary across specialties and library types about who we are. Finding a cohesive message of "us" is difficult enough at a micro level and becomes nearly impossible when we start looking at the profession as a whole. Yet, this inability to define ourselves, in a targeted way, is precisely what makes it nearly impossible to share what we do to a broader audience. If we cannot articulate and agree what the librarian brand is, how can we expect others to know or care about what we have to offer? True powerhouse librarians know that having an identifiable brand is the first step in selling our services. To find the threads that connect us, we must be willing to focus on what brings our profession together versus how our specialties make us unique. I would argue that every library (and thus librarian) strives to do the following:

- Serve
- Educate
- Provide access
- Build community
- Advocate

How we do these things and where our specific role fits in may vary. But the end goals are the same, and this is what unites us.

Working to build a professional identity and brand is the first step librarians need to take before we can begin educating the masses about what we have to offer. Why? Our message needs to be clear and unified. Without a targeted message, our significance will be lost in the white noise of the details. And, librarian reality check, at this stage the details mostly don't matter to anyone but us. The hard reality is, if we are continually needing to address outdated notions of who we are, then we will not have the bandwidth to change in the ways we need to stay relevant. We cannot be relevant if nobody understands our value. Worse, we cannot begin to develop the flexible mind-set needed to reimagine ourselves if we are continually struggling with who we are. The image crisis stops here.

Below are the powerhouse steps we can use to start addressing this situation in a constructive manner. Beware—these steps are not for the faint of heart. This process will require a lot of professional soul searching and a willingness to clearly see ourselves—warts and all. It may not be pretty. But we'll be better for it as a profession. To start, the discussion and changes must be as follows:

Librarian Driven

Change is hard. Even desired changes take time to achieve. If there is truly going to be a long-term impact on the profession, our image has to be developed from the ground up. That means taking a good, hard look at the past, present, and future. It means having open, honest, supported conversations about legacy thinking and attitudes. It means picking a course, taking action, and actually making changes rather than passively debating the issue. We already have a great small-scale example of our ability to do this in our move from print to digital collections. Only then will there be the buy-in and momentum needed to drive the large-scale change that is needed.

From a Place of Empowerment

It can be easy to feel disempowered and grumpy when users don't know we are degreed professionals, and faculty don't realize we hold equal rank. Rebranding ourselves is also our opportunity for reeducation. Librarians bring a unique skill set all our own to the table. We need to recognize our part as collaborators and own it, rather than just being happy that stakeholders remembered the library exists. We are what we project. So let's make sure it rocks.

Informed

We need to actually converse with our stakeholders early on in the professional identity conversation. We need to know how they are viewing us, how they are identifying our roles, and the most vital pieces to retain. Working from assumptions rather than data will undermine the whole process. If our rebranding is completely disconnected from how the world values us, then we have missed our opportunity to make a meaningful and lasting impression. There are no second chances for a comeback.

Reflected in MLIS Education

Change needs to happen at all levels. However, how we recruit and train future professionals is the lifeblood of a successful image overhaul. We can no longer only be focused on developing "hard" skill sets for the future (digitization, for example). MLIS programs also need to be educated about the "soft skills" needed to be successful long term. Disruptions across multiple fields have opened up a competitive market for what used to be library "territory." Programs need to start accounting for how the next generation can continue to market our skills, manage change, and acquire leadership abilities. We need to be purposely identifying and recruiting those with the aptitude to be flexible, creative problem solvers who recognize that the library is about knowledge not books!

Embrace Business (No . . . Seriously)

The idea of libraries as business is a tough one to swallow for many in the field. However, there is way more overlap in our services, models, and processes than most of us admit. Libraries across the spectrum are now becoming accountable for showing our return on investment to our governing bodies. We tailor our services to match patron (aka customer) needs and wants to keep our usage up. Concepts such as process improvement, quality improvement, agile design, and strategic planning are making their way into more and more librarians' vocabulary. We need to stop kidding ourselves and realize to be successful requires us to embrace some of what the business world has to offer. That is not to say we need to abandon the mission and ideals libraries were founded on. However, we must be open to identifying and adapting smart business practices to compete with the new crop of competing industries. If we continue to ignore this truth, we will always be two steps behind.

Without conscious efforts to start unifying the library profession we run the risk of fracturing ourselves into nonexistence. Although branding is the first step, we must also make a commitment to reexamine the way we define ourselves. This leads us to . . .

REFRAME OUR THINKING

Part of the reason the "that's not my job" reference is so rampant is because in our desire to specialize we have assigned ourselves very specific hats. Job descriptions are incredibly helpful constructions to define what it is we're supposed to be evaluated on. They give us responsibility, authority, a set of expectations, and at the end of the year a neat little box to check off that we've contributed to the organization in a specific way. Hello merit! The problem with this construction is that although everything is very neat, proper, and organized it can be limiting in how we see ourselves. We start to think of ourselves as what is written versus what we employ to accomplish it. Our focus becomes on what we do—not how we do it. This way of thinking immediately focuses on the no. The true powerhouse librarian's goal is to get to yes.

Getting to yes requires us to stop and evaluate the big picture. It demands that each person know his or her personal assets and how exactly to use them. Essentially this process is all about reflection and finding a new way to talk about ourselves. Seems simple enough, right? Then why is it so hard to get colleagues to think in these terms? Quite simply, it threatens the status quo. Job titles are neat. Job descriptions are focused (theoretically). Skill sets? Well those can be applied to almost anything. It becomes much harder to argue "that's not my job" when you have the skill set to do it.

Now to be fair, there are plenty of librarians who don't mind messing with the status quo. The issue, to my mind, more lies within the change management cycle. One of the basic premises of change theory is that people fear the unknown (Jones and Recardo 2013). It is the fear of an unquantifiable outcome we're battling, not the actual modification itself. The shift to viewing ourselves through skill sets is challenging because it creates a vastness for opportunities that cannot be immediately defined. The fear that we could be asked to do "anything" without recourse is what keeps many of us up at night. Fear not, good friends. This is precisely why having a cohesive brand to fall back on is so important. Strong branding helps to build those parameters explicitly. Expectations are already set to some point. Having a cohesive and recognizable brand that is mindful of our patron experiences outlines the conversation from the very beginning (Spring, Carbone, and Haeckel 2002). Additionally, people are generally smart enough to recognize the importance context plays in relation to skill. Unconvinced? Think about it this way. When was the last time you went to the dog groomers to get a haircut? Although it's a similar skill set, the context is very different. Good branding equals context. A focus on skill sets equals organizational agility.

Another reason refocusing on our toolkit rather than our titles is imperative is the increasing speed in which disruptive forces are hitting the information landscape. Publishing, technology, government policy, funding, health care, education, and communication models are all radically transforming.

Each shift causes a new wrinkle for how we must consider and respond to our stakeholders. Working from a traditional mental framework does not allow the kind of fluidity needed to respond rapidly. Our users' expectations and needs are influenced by these shifts. Their questions and requests for assistance are insights into their needs, and more importantly their wants. Voids signal an untapped opportunity to remarket ourselves. Libraries would do well to capitalize on that. If we don't someone else will.

"That's not my job" or "that isn't in my job description." Both statements that get my dander up. I know that in some cases union rules do prohibit some things, but usually what is being asked is tied to the mission of the library and institution. When someone says it isn't their job I usually reply with maybe not exactly but this patron needs our help, so can we make an exception this time? Aren't they why we are here? No students, no us.

I started in the hospitality industry, specifically hotels. I have a different opinion of customer service that other people. My responses to patron requests tend to be a little more patron focused. I compare being a librarian to working in the shoe department at Nordstrom. The person walked in wanting information (shoes), and we need to help them get what they want and do it in the best way we can so that they come back and use us again. If you treat them poorly or make it hard on them, they won't come back. And that is not a successful library. (KT)

BUILDING OUR SKILL TOOLKITS

The beauty of focusing on building skills versus just performing a job function is that your toolkit can be uniquely customized. Skills can be deployed in any number of ways. They can be expanded to offer custom value-added services. Think about the following. "Executes vendor contacts" is a very specific library task. It is a function that any content-focused librarian would need to be able to perform. Switching to a skill set mentality, what that task is actually asking us to do is negotiate effectively. Suddenly the world on what that ability can be used for has opened up dramatically. The skill of negotiation can be used to deal with vendor contracts, unions, consortiums, facilitating meetings, multistakeholder space planning, event planning, settling interpersonal conflicts, and so forth. It can be applied in any number of useful ways. Who says the library couldn't offer a workshop on contract negotiation? We have in-house experts who utilize that skill every day! More often than not though, the function or title we use obscures the bigger picture. The people responsible for "training" are not necessarily the same people doing the "negotiating." Unless your library actively tries to cross-pollinate work units, it is possible that these two groups have little overlap on a regular basis. Staying in our role-based thinking can hinder us from exploring how we could best profit from the diverse abilities within our organizations.

Toolkits are ever expanding. With that expansion comes the ability to reassemble and reconfigure our in-house teams based off of the need at the moment. Imagine the impact libraries could have if we were able to translate our skills across functions to serve our patrons accordingly. There are already great examples out there to study. Solo librarians perform in this way every day! Below is a list of standard job responsibilities and their associated skills to get you started thinking about what might be in your toolkit (a full worksheet is included at the end of the chapter). Examples for how a job description might translate into the language of skills include the following:

Job Description	Examples of Skills
Effectively teaches content to students	defining objectives, sets learning outcomes
Executes searches	strategy building, understanding of taxonomies
Seeks out extramural funding	grant writing, budget development
Manages the circulation department	supervision of staff, scheduling, ILS experience
Develops the print/electronic collection	license negotiation, relationship building

The combinations found within a single library could be limitless. Imagine the possibilities! Building a library where people can use their entire repertoire of abilities to fulfill the organization's mission is the ultimate dream. Making that dream a reality is the obvious next step.

Now that you see how productive a skill set focus can be, how do we start getting our organizations in a place where this way of thinking

Important Tip

When thinking about skill sets it is important to remember that interest plays a strong role. Although someone may have a particular aptitude for something, if they find it boring or uninteresting most likely they won't want to do it. Make sure to understand people's passions and find a balance between need and desire to ensure lasting motivation.

becomes the norm? The most efficient way to start moving in this direction is to know your organization's goals, what the potential barriers are to getting there, and what assets you have at your disposal. Armed with this knowledge, from there you can start laying the groundwork for promoting the cultural change needed to support this kind of outlook. Do not, I repeat, *do not* start this kind of change work without having a clear understanding of your organization and its culture. Your messaging will need to be spot on, and if you do not have a clear understanding of how things "work around here," your opportunity to advocate and influence will be lost. To effectively lay the groundwork for this kind of shift, start by doing the following:

- Create channels for communication across departments, units, teams, and so forth. Silos will kill this type of effort and should be vigilantly watched for and nipped in the bud as quickly as possible.
- Get leadership support early. Cultures don't just happen. Leaders must be actively involved in shifting an organization's mentality.
- Enlist experts when and where you can. HR professionals, change-management consultants, behavioral psychology professors, and so on, are all well "tuned in" to what makes people tick. If you have access to these assets use them. Unless you're an expert on human behavior, getting outside help on dos, don'ts, can'ts, and won'ts will be paramount for your success.
- Work to create buy-in. Get people involved in the conversation at the beginning. You may not be able to have complete consensus, but at least people will have the opportunity to share their feedback and feel heard.
- Anticipate setbacks, and find ways to mentally prepare yourself to keep pushing forward. Eliciting change is a marathon, not a sprint. Mentally prepare for the long haul.

Important Tip

When evaluating roles and skill sets, it also helps to consider whether or not a different profession might need to be recruited altogether. For instance, someone with an MBA or marketing degree could be really helpful in overseeing a process such as strategic planning or designing a fundraising campaign.

Getting people to reframe how they see themselves will require a well-thought-out, sustained effort. True powerhouse librarians know they will need to engage beyond just conversations. Specific targets that can be achieved and measured will need to be implemented. To ensure a lasting vision and dialogue around the move from roles to skill sets, consideration of past, present, and future toolkits will need to be part of the conversation. With the endless mash-up comes the need to recognize when particular skills need to be acquired, updated, or retired. Skill sets offer the chance to bring a commitment to lifelong learning to life.

STAYING CURRENT

Positioning ourselves to determine next-generation skills can be a tricky business. It will require a vigilant monitoring of current trends (both external to the library and within our spaces) and anticipation of future pathways. Focusing on toolkits or skills provides us advantages in staying ahead of the game in the following ways:

- Acquiring skills can be planned for at both short- and long-range intervals.
- People expect to update or acquire skills more regularly than changing roles.
- Toolkits offer unthreatening language to discuss personnel planning for the present and future.
- Skill sets implicitly imply change but with a focus on the benefit for the individual as well as the library.

If we are continually focused on how to do our jobs better, rather than what we are doing at the moment, it becomes easier to embrace our next incarnation. The threat of irrelevance or not being valued is lessened, so we can focus on today, knowing we are also preparing for tomorrow step by step. Skill sets allow us to make small, preparatory changes at a sustained pace. The anxiety of change is managed because it is happening regularly and allows for small (rather than sweeping) corrections. A focus on skill sets empowers us to manage the change around us, rather than being managed by outside forces.

We all know that what it means to be a librarian today will be different twenty years from now. Part of what is so scary for many of us is that it is difficult to know what exactly we need to embrace and what we should be releasing. By the time we're finally comfortable enough to move a service out of beta, the world is already wanting version 2.0. This reality is captured nicely in the sentiment that "many disconnections between the library and millennial generation are closely related to infrastructure[;] the library is not that seamless, instantly available, networked information environment" (Widén and Kronqvist-Berg 2014, p. 3). We try to be as networked and tech savvy as possible, but at our core the library is about service, not technology.

One of the biggest challenges currently facing the profession is trying to figure out where we belong in the digital landscape. Although there are some indications of what areas may still be relevant in years to come (digitization, for example), there are still needs yet to be discovered. It can be difficult to plan accordingly when the trajectory has yet to be fully set. In their research on the future librarian, Gunilla Widén and Maria Kronqvist-Berg (2014) highlighted several key competencies or skill areas that they anticipated continuing forward. These skills focused squarely on IT, pedagogy, communication, collection management, and research environments. Happily, these are all areas that are already firmly entrenched into our present library fabric.

The challenge for those looking to build their toolkit for the future is identifying which force will exert the most pressure. Social, political, and economic factors are all influencing the work we do. The Affordable Care Act brought the focus on public libraries as places to learn about health-care insurance options and access the various health-care portals. Medical libraries struggle to help their institutions meet meaningful use standards. Academic libraries are trying to understand how to support transitions from independent medical centers to accountable care networks. These

Five Good Skill Habits to Cultivate

- Update your toolkit regularly.
- Identify foundation skills versus translation skills.
- Find skill partners you can work with to build complementary toolkits.
- Make sure to practice using your skills once they are acquired.
- Be willing to develop skills in areas others aren't.

Five Skill Habits to Avoid

- Undermarketing unique skills you have
- Building skills in only one area
- Avoiding developing new skills altogether
- Acquiring a skill only in name (e.g., you took a class and never actually applied what you learned)
- Blocking others from acquiring a skill because it doesn't fit what they are doing "today"

are by no means traditional library roles. However, our skill sets made it possible for the library to rise up and meet the challenge that this type of policy change put forth.

PARTING THOUGHTS

Libraries have reached a critical moment in our professional history. Influences from every direction have culminated in an unclear professional identity. This identity crisis has helped to create confusion on the part of our users about what exactly the library does. Rethinking and reframing ourselves has become a necessity to ensure we remain relevant.

Developing a strong library brand, accepted and shared at a professional level, is the only way to guarantee our future. Like so many other industries, we need to realize what our value is and articulate it in a way that sticks. Without this cohesive image to guide us forward, we risk losing our important place in the "information market" to those information professionals driven by profit.

Rebranding is only half the battle though. To stay competitive and agile, finding a new way to think about our roles is needed. Focusing on building our professional toolkits with skills rather than defining ourselves based on our job descriptions is a key component to success. Where skill sets can be molded, adjusted, and deployed to solve any problem, viewing ourselves within the confines of our job function is limiting and prescriptive. The future will require us to be responsive beyond what we have seen so far. Concentrating on our unique skills and strengths can help us to stay in an agile state of mind.

SKILL SET INVENTORY

The goal of this inventory is to help you identify what skills you have developed related to a variety of standard library functions. List any specialized skills that may be unique within the library under the "other" section.

Teaching:

Research:

Systems:

Technical services:

Content:

Administration:

Leadership:

Business processes:

Communications:

Advancement:

Facilities:

Other:

REFERENCES

Berry, Leonard L., Lewis P. Carbone, and Stephan H. Haeckel. 2002. "Managing the Total Customer Experience." *MIT Sloan Management Review* 43 (3): 85–89.

Dorabjee, Shaida. 2015. "All Change: The Workplace Culture Challenge." *CILIP Update*, July/August, 41–43.

Grant, Carl. 2015. "It's Time to Define a New Brand for Libraries: Let's Make Sure It Leaves People Soaring, Not Snoring." *Public Library Quarterly* 34 (2): 99–106.

Jones, David J., and Ronald J. Recardo. 2013. *Leading and Implementing Business Change Management*. New York: Routledge.

Lord, Simon. 2014. "Closing the Gap: The Five Essential Attributes of the Modern Information Professional." *Legal Information Management* 14 (4): 258–65.

Shill, Harold B., and Shawn Tonner. 2003. "Creating a Better Place: Physical Improvements in Academic Libraries, 1995–2002." *College and Research Libraries* 64 (6): 431–66.

Somerville, Mary M., and Margaret Brown-Sica. 2011. "Library Space Planning: A Participatory Action Research Approach." *Electronic Library* 29 (5): 669–81.

Widén, Gunilla, and Maria Kronqvist-Berg. 2014. "The Future Librarian: A Diverse and Complex Professional." *Proceedings of the IATUL Conferences*, paper 7. https://docs.lib.purdue.edu/.

10

Cultivating Attitude
Gracefully Handling Setbacks and Sidestepping Burnout

How This Might Look in Practice:

- Hold "postmortem" sessions for big library projects or impactful events to help identify what went well and also air any disappointments.
- Identify and share easy-to-do wellness activities (e.g., chair stretches) in shared staff spaces such as the break room.

Picture this: your new service is on the brink of being launched. You've mapped out the whole concept, spent time building up a support team, engaged the right stakeholders, and learned the right skills. Victory is about to be yours when the unforeseeable happens. The economy crashes, there is an unplanned change in leadership, someone takes ill, or a new priority emerges that requires your immediate attention. In other words, the proverbial rug has been pulled out from underneath you, and you my friend have hit a setback.

Unforeseen roadblocks and setbacks are a major part of today's work environment. Depending on the type of library you find yourself in, the daily flow can very much be "here today, gone tomorrow." This is not a phenomenon unique to libraries. Changes in technology, connectedness, information, and expectation have all contributed to the modern work landscape for most industries including education, health care, and technology. Learning how to cultivate an attitude that allows you to gracefully

accept setbacks while continuing to persevere is the final step into blossoming into a total powerhouse librarian.

This final chapter will be dedicated to helping you learn how to cope
with the unexpected in a positive and fruitful manner. Although there is
no controlling the universe, there are certain outlooks and activities you
can do to continue shining your light when you or those around you are
faced with adversity.

LOSE THE 'TUDE

There is a lot of truth to the old adage that the only thing you can control is your attitude. The concept of attitude has been discussed over
the years in a number of different ways and is central to the study of
social psychology. In their chapter discussing attitude, as part of *The
Handbook of Social Psychology*, authors Alice Eagly and Shelly Chaiken describe an attitude as "a psychological tendency that is expressed
by evaluating a particular entity with some degree of favor or disfavor"
(1998, 269). According to them, essentially we typically feel positively
or negatively toward an object, person, or situation. This definition seems
simple enough. However, simple does not take into account the number
of forces acting on and shaping us each day. People are complex and
always evolving, and life is always filled with a hundred different shades
of gray. In his discussion on the differences between attitudes, opinions,
and values, Manfred Bergman makes some interesting observations on
how attitudes are impacted by what he describes as key drivers. In his
discussion he notes the following:

> In terms of attitudes' impact on constraining behavior, it is important to
> consider not only attitude structures, but also their relative strength, which
> has been studied extensively under the heading of attitude dimensions (e.g.,
> Krosnick et al. 1993). Attitude *extremity*, for instance, relates to how much
> an object is liked or disliked, or how far away it is from a hypothetical
> neutral point with reference to its affective evaluation. The degree to which
> people evaluate their confidence in their attitude's correctness is measured
> in terms of *certainty*. *Importance* or *centrality* describes how important or
> central an attitude is to the individual. Attitude strength also varies accord-
> ing to available *knowledge* of the attitude object, as well as an individual's

interest in acquiring such knowledge. *Salience* and *accessibility* refer to the degree to which an attitude is present in one's everyday social perception and social interaction. Attitude strength has also been studied in terms of *direct experience* of the attitude object, as well as the extent to which an attitude or an attitude object is affectively and cognitively *consistent* with other attitudes and attitude objects. (Bergman 1998, 85)

So in stepping back and looking at both Bergman and Eagly and Chaiken together, we start getting a more layered understanding of attitudes that looks something like the following: As people, we possess something equivalent to an internal Likert scale that swings somewhere between positive and negative depending on the stimulus before us. This stimulus can be a person, place, action, object, situation, and so forth. The stimulus itself can be neutral. However, given the way we identify with certain variables such as knowledge, accessibility, extremity, and direct experience, we will sway our attitude toward one side or the other.

Clearly predicting attitudes is virtually an impossible task. People are too uniquely formulated to be able to accurately calculate where their attitude on any given topic might fall. Just think about how many times you yourself may have been surprised by your own attitude about something. However, knowing that our brains tend to slide back and forth on our own internal scale gives you the power to make adjustments.

Like so many things in life, our attitudes do not have to be permanent. We can fine-tune our scales to swing more toward the positive. How can we do this? To start with, you will need a firm understanding of your own personal tendencies—that is, our old friend self-awareness. Additional contributors such as positivity, gratitude, mindfulness, resilience, and action can have a profound impact on cultivating a winning attitude.

KNOW THYSELF (PART DEUX)

Back in chapter 2 we touched upon knowing yourself well enough to take risks effectively. Developing a keen understanding of what makes you tick is also a key element in cultivating the ability to take things in stride. Self-reflection is a necessary step in developing your ability to both self-regulate and bounce back. By allotting time to inventory and

evaluate your natural tendencies, preferences, and the results your responses elicited gives you a clear indication into what type of work you
may have to undertake to reshape your outlook.

I know, I know—we're evaluating ourselves again, you might cry. My
answer to you is yes—the time it takes to self-reflect and understand your
motivations, likes, dislikes, and responses is time well spent. Why? Without knowing your attitude habits, it will be difficult to make any kind of
sustained change needed for long-term success. "But I've already got a
good attitude," you might think. My question to you then is, how well do
you keep that good attitude when things turn out different than expected?
Do you roll with and embrace the challenge fairly quickly, or does it cause
a negative ripple effect for the duration of the experience?

The goal of taking time to self-reflect is not to create judgments on
whether or not you tend to be more optimistic or pessimistic. Knowing
your natural comfort zone can help you develop tricks to catch yourself
when you need to reframe or readjust your mental framework. Below is
a quick reflective activity to get you thinking about where your mental
habits might fall.

You're laying in a field of tall grass, enjoying a gentle summer breeze
and deep, warm sunshine. The field itself is wide and expansive, dotted
with an occasional oak tree and containing a small stone wall several
feet wide. The experience has been so peaceful and comfortable you're
on the verge of falling asleep. Just as you doze off, big, fat raindrops
start falling from the sky. The sun is still shining, but you are now in the
middle of a classic summer sunstorm. Rain hadn't been forecasted for
the day, so you had walked to the field and did not bring an umbrella.
You do have a blanket, but the walk back to shelter will take some time.
What comes next?

Take a moment to jot down any initial thoughts, feelings, scenes, or re-
actions. Now evaluate what you wrote, paying particular emphasis to the
tone. What do you notice? Was your reaction, solution, experience, and
next scene slanted more toward the positive or negative? Perhaps it was
a mix of both. Why? The point of this activity is not to get you to judge
yourself and your reaction to the scene but to help you identify why you
may have interpreted a fairly neutral experience in positive or negative
terms. We all carry personal bias that shades our world and our interactions in it. Know it, recognize it, and use it to your advantage.

Important Tip

It is important to remember that our attitudes may be impacted by current events we are experiencing. Taking time to consistently reflect using a technique such as journaling or peer feedback with a trusted friend can help you gauge out of the normal personal fluctuations.

THE POWER OF THE POSITIVE

While it is important to know your natural neutral zone, take heart that there is plenty that you can do to swing your pendulum toward the sunny side of the street. Much attention has been paid in recent years to the new study of happiness or positive psychology. In a nutshell, positive psychology studies how well-being impacts all facets of the individual, including health, wellness, happiness, and success (Azar 2011). In her study entitled "The Six Essentials of Workplace Positivity," author Elizabeth Cabrera defines positivity as "the frequent experience of positive emotions such as joy, hope, gratitude, interest, serenity and inspiration" (Cabrera 2012, 51). It is important to note that the descriptors in her definition all relate to behavior or emotions that lead to a certain level of satisfaction or happiness. Why is this important if you are looking to get things done? Take a minute to reflect on those librarians you deem to be most successful; would you categorize them as typically positive or negative people? My guess would be they land more on the positive side of things. This observation is important for several reasons.

Little can be achieved without the support or assistance of others. Both negativity and positivity can be catching. Just look at how often one team member's foul mood can create a cloud over a whole meeting. It is my experience that working with someone who approaches things from a positive place from the onset puts you in a better position to achieve results, oftentimes at less expense. Still not convinced? Think about it. How much do you generally need to convince people who are happy and positive to do any of the following:

- Get on board for a new assignment (generate buy-in)
- Volunteer to assist with extra work, problems that arise, or learning something new

- Find faster approaches to completing tasks or meeting deadlines
- Help nudge team members to stay on track or push through when challenges arise
- Create a bit of fun (even in tense situations), which helps foster creativity or collaboration

I would argue, all of these scenarios directly contribute to getting things accomplished. It becomes pretty powerful to see how often having a positive attitude can save our projects or institutions time and resources (translation—money $$) by fostering in-house creativity, commitment, and problem solving. Relating the power of positivity directly to the workplace, Cabrera notes, "Research shows that the more positive emotions people experience, the more successful they are. Positive employees make better decisions, are more creative, more productive, more resilient and have better interpersonal skills. Companies can, therefore, gain a competitive advantage by creating positive work environments" (2012, 51). Seems pretty intuitive, right? So then why can this be such a challenge?

Staying positive takes work. We are constantly faced with a barrage of stories and situations that focus on loss, violence, fear, and change. According to the media, both mass and social, we walk on a knife's edge of catastrophe every day. If that is true, then of course being positive takes work! If you're suddenly feeling defeated, take heart; there is good news. Although it is thought that approximately 50 percent of positivity is related to our genetic makeup, the other 50 percent we have direct control over. Out of that 50 percent, a small portion of our positivity is related to our circumstances. However, the vast majority (about 40 percent) can be directly attributed to our thoughts and actions (Cabrera 2012). We have total control over a lot more than we are often given credit for. The next few sections can help you start to gain mastery over your own thoughts or actions in an intentional way.

Important Tip

Gaining self-awareness and creating sustainable changes in your attitude require continued work. You will likely need to revisit these activities time and time again. Know that some times will be easier than others based on outside circumstances. But you will succeed!

GRATITUDE

The *Oxford English Dictionary* defines the word *gratitude* as "the quality of being thankful." Take a moment to reread that definition. Do any words stand out? If you selected the words *quality* and *being*, give yourself a gold star. I focus on these two words not because the term *thankful* isn't important but because both words are actionable and completely within your individual control. It is one thing to say you're thankful but quite another to "be" thankful. Similarly, qualities are characteristics that one can intentionally work to develop. Our worlds are shaped by our actions and inactions; the lens we choose to view situations through; and the meanings we attach to circumstances. The ability to weave gratitude into our daily interactions can have a profound effect on the situations we find ourselves in.

Take a moment and think about the last time you were grateful for something.

- What effect did that feeling have on you?
- How did it color your outlook after the fact?

Now take a moment and answer the following:

- Did that feeling lead to any actions on your part?
- How were those actions similar or dissimilar to what actions you might normally take?

True powerhouse librarians know that developing the ability to translate the feeling of gratitude into small gestures can motivate those around you to continue offering assistance, support, and the willingness to partner. Why? We are biologically wired to desire acceptance and companionship. What demonstrates you are an important member of the team more than having someone recognize and appreciate your contribution? Conversely, how quickly do we become demoralized when our efforts go unnoticed or we feel undervalued? Demonstrating gratitude for the roles people play, input they provide, or experience they lend to a project are motivators that go far beyond money.

Gratitude can also be a powerful tool to employ when a setback is encountered both within ourselves and with others. Finding what you are thankful for in a tough situation can be really difficult. If it wasn't, then disappointments wouldn't be so disappointing. But cultivating gratitude, first internally and then within the environment around you, can help you identify important lessons that can be translated into future success. If done right, gratitude can help deliver a one-two pick-me-up when the going gets tough. For instance, personal gratitude (so internally focused) can help you identify the lesson you needed to learn to enhance your personal growth (insert individual laundry list here). Most often this type of learning tends to be of the picking ourselves back up variety. Or as I like to think of it, how not to approach a situation again scenario. The gratitude piece is tied to not necessarily the specific situation in question but often the opportunity to do it better the next time. If you have taken the time to share your attitude of gratitude with those around you, often those lucky individuals will be the first ones there offering support to help lift you back up. This type of outlook and energy is contagious and fuels the chance for success more than ambition alone.

If approaching life with gratitude doesn't come naturally to you, don't fear. The following activities are small changes you can implement to work gratitude into your daily interactions.

Gratitude Lists

This is a quick reflective practice that can be used to start or end your day. Set a certain number of acts or fortunes to recognize, and take a few moments to routinely reflect and identify them. There is no need to only focus on positive interactions (although these are usually the easiest to readily identify). Oftentimes there are valuable insights to be drawn from difficulties are well. Lists can be compiled to revisit later, said out loud, or quietly thought about. A sample list might look something like this: today I am grateful for a patron unexpectedly thanking me for good service, fresh-baked chocolate-chip cookies, and the bus running on time. The point is not to focus on grand gestures but to find and appreciate the simple things throughout your day.

Say Thank You

To me, this phrase has become undervalued in our fast-paced, technology-centric world. It is amazing how much punch a simple, genuine word of thanks can have on those around you. Recognizing the impact of the small things people do for us can go a long way toward creating gratitude in yourself and those around you. In our culture of expectation, taking a moment to acknowledge the assistance you receive sends a strong message that you value what someone has to offer.

Once Again, Enlist a Buddy

Sometimes it can be difficult to maintain an outlook of gratitude when life gets hectic or we face a number of challenges at once. Having a person who can mirror gratitude back to you can be an invaluable touchstone to bring attentions back in line.

Cultivating gratitude takes work but is achievable with regular practice. Although not an overnight fix for many obstacles, developing gratitude can help you to focus on what's right when things go wrong. This shift in attention can make challenges feel more solvable by giving you a more balanced picture of the problem at hand.

MINDFULNESS; OR, THE ART OF BEING PRESENT

In addition to approaching situations with gratitude, being fully immersed in the moment can help stave off the feeling of being overwhelmed when things get tough. Mindfulness is essentially the ability to set your focus to the present and experience the here and now (Beard 2014). Although the principle sounds simple enough, mastering your awareness can sometimes feel like herding a rogue litter of feral cats.

Most people spend their time either reviewing and reliving the past or planning for how they expect the future to go. Both outlets can create an escape from the reality that is the present. Often we use the past to impart meaning onto what is happening in our current situation (Beard 2014). Likewise, we regularly daydream about the future to envision what might be. Although neither orientation is especially bad or good, both outlooks take us away from experiencing the here and now. When we get too focused on the past or future it becomes easy to feel overwhelmed, conflicted, burnt out, or fearful, all of which can impede your ability to get things done. Engaging in mindfulness can help you step back from those feelings and focus on the task at hand.

One of the hallmarks of our profession is the appreciation for tradition. Libraries and librarians continually struggle to find balance between what was versus what is. Oftentimes the past is used as a gauge to determine future success. You hear this when you bring ideas to library colleagues and they say things such as, "we tried something like that two years, and it didn't work because . . ." This is a common scene for many of us in the library world. Carrying those past failures to the present can undermine your ability to take action, because it may obscure the present reality. This is not to say we should completely forget past practice. There are always some useful takeaways that can be implemented to make success more likely. However, by being focused on the present (today), you are likely to see that many things have changed from that past failure. For instance, you may have new personnel, resources, mandates, skill sets, needs, and so forth, that were not available previously. By staying in the present, you can honor what was without being trapped by it.

Getting to that place where you are present will take a generous amount of practice. Below are some tricks you can try to keep you and your colleagues from wandering too far into the past or future:

Frame your conversations. It is always a good idea to sit down and look at the information you have at hand. I like to think of it as the "what do we know" game. Likely there will be details that are both in the past and forthcoming. Pool all of those pearls of information needs together. But instead of getting bogged down in the history or the "what ifs" of the future, focus on what that means for the work that needs to be accomplished today. By focusing on creating actions based on the here and now, you are less likely to have unproductive conversations focusing on uncontrollables.

Find a mantra. A mantra is something you can refer back to over and over. Oftentimes, it is a phrase that you can repeat continually to tune other things out and quiet the mind. In our case, the mantra really only needs to be asked once but should bring your thoughts or the conversation back to the present. I personally like the phrase "In this moment I/we know" or "In this moment I am." These phrases refocus attention to the present and also set you up for potential action.

IF AT FIRST YOU DON'T SUCCEED

Everyone always loves a good comeback story. We herald those who come from humble beginnings and work their way up to the top. We applaud the troubled actor who is able to return from the edge and win the Oscar. Resilience is a key factor in succeeding and a common theme in those stories the public loves so much.

Although resilience can be considered a trait, if you really think about it, the foundation of resilience is interlinked with both belief and attitude. In her book *Mindset: The New Psychology of Success*, Dr. Carol S. Dweck discusses the growth versus fixed mind-set. She describes the fixed mind-set as "believing that your qualities are carved in stone" (2007, 10). She contends that this type of mind-set "creates an urgency to prove yourself over and over again" (10). Essentially, those who hold this outlook believe that what we are born with is what we've got, period. As a contrast, Dweck posits that a "*growth mindset* is based on the belief that your basic qualities are things that you can cultivate through your efforts. Although people may differ in every which way—in their initial talents, aptitudes, interest or temperaments—everyone can change and grow though application and experience" (7). In other words, how we choose to view ourselves (as either fully formed or always growing) plays a large role in how we approach and respond to situations.

If our inherent belief and attitude is that failure is personal, then every failure will be a reflection of who we are (or aren't). Although we personally may be a contributor in that failure, it is likely that there were other important elements at play. Being able to see the whole picture is the foundational basis for developing resiliency. For example, take a moment to consider factors such as the following:

- Timing. Was your library in the midst of trying to implement multiple changes at once? Was there a change in leadership? Or perhaps did priorities shift due to outside influences?

Important Tip

There is a difference between reflecting and dwelling. If you find you are unable to identify important takeaways, you are most likely dwelling rather than objectively reflecting.

- Resources. Did your library suddenly face a budget cut? Were key personnel reallocated to other projects? Did costs suddenly skyrocket due to unforeseen circumstances?
- Personal. Did you have a change in your personal life beyond your control such as an illness? Did your priorities shift to accommodate an unanticipated work project?

More than likely there were multiple reasons for the setback you faced, a number of them outside of your control. If you can step back and try to identify all of the factors at play, then you can try to preempt those pitfalls before they happen the next time. Resiliency is about identifying a way to move forward—even when the path may not be clear at the onset.

LESS CONVERSATION, MORE ACTION

Action—that thing that so many of us want to see happen, yet so seldom does. What is it that stops us in the library world from being able to act? For some, it can be enough to simply ponder the possibilities. Temperament (both personal and professional) likely holds a great deal of influence here. Librarianship tends to draw many with the thinker, strategizer mentality (Williamson and Lounsbury 2016). When you live in the realm of ideas, oftentimes contemplating the principles of that idea is enough to feel gratification. The excitement lives in the conception. However, inaction is the antithesis of any powerhouse librarian who is trying to get things done. Why? Without action, we are unable to share our brilliant ideas with others in the community, let alone in a meaningful way. Meaning for libraries is created by evaluating impact. Impact at its core implies action.

Too often in our profession action becomes overly intertwined with risk. We feel we must identify and calculate every possible angle before even a baby step can be made. This is good in theory but not always realistic or beneficial. I beg you to stop the insanity! If you find that risk is still holding you back, revisit chapter 2. If you're ready to start moving forward, even if it is only a walking dead–paced shuffle, the following tips are for you:

Realize inaction is still an action. Depending on the situation, the inability to act can be just as detrimental as action without reflection. Truthfully, you make just as much of a statement by what you choose to forgo as what you undertake. Evaluate the message your inaction is sending as you would the pitfalls of a specific game plan.

Dead ends are still helpful. Sometimes we have to travel down a lot of roads before finding the right one. Taking wrong turns can help you pinpoint why something finally went right and provide sound argument for a particular course of action.

Action is addictive. We can't learn to trust our instincts without testing them out. Once we get used to action it becomes easier to overcome, say, self-, bureaucratic, or institutional inertia.

There is nothing more gratifying than being able to show a real tangible product that you have created. Action, from the conception process to the final unveiling, is a necessary part of the process to achieving success. Think about it, have you ever heard a "success" story where action wasn't part of the equation? Committing to act, even if it is microsteps, such as putting something on your to-do list, is a key ingredient to blossoming into the powerhouse you are.

Important Tip

Personal responsibility is an important part of being resilient. There may be contributing factors beyond your control that contribute to failures. However, identifying your role is just as important. Exerting authority over what you can, when you can, or identifying how to do something better is essential to any powerhouse librarian's success.

Five Good Attitude Habits to Cultivate

- Reflect often.
- Find an attitude buddy.
- Try to see the whole picture to find connections rather than focusing on a piece of the situation.
- Surround yourself with inspiration in the form of notes, pictures, quotes, and so forth.
- Remove *can't* from your vocabulary.

Five Attitude Habits to Avoid

- Lengthy wallowing
- Ignoring how outside influences, such as people and the environment, are impacting you
- Negative self-talk
- Believing things will never change (good or bad)
- Working in absolutes

I have always wanted to be a library director. My first professional job was at a nonprofit institution. I was there ten years. I moved up the ranks; I thought I was well on my way to being a director. I had risen to the position of operations supervisor (their version of assistant director). I thought I was ready to be a director. Once I started looking at job openings, applying, and interviewing, [it] turns out I was not where hiring institutions wanted me to be. I was really heartbroken, mentally set back. I figured my goal might never happen. I eventually took a position as a department head, which felt to me like a step backward. However, I was lucky enough to end up working for a fabulous director, a woman who really helped me get what I needed to push forward to my goal. In fact, she sent me the job opening for my current assistant director position at a different institution. I still want to be a director. I know it will happen. She really helped me get my confidence back.

Burnout is not a fun position to find yourself in. I've been there more than once, for different reasons. In some cases you can't prevent it. If your library is shorthanded and you have too much on your plate, you will burn out. If you aren't challenged enough by the work you do, you can also get burnout. Family and friends are a good source of help: people to talk to, have fun with. Finding hobbies and making time for them. I actually have a really hard time with that. I need to make time to do these things I enjoy; they will help me have balance and keep me from burnout. Also, in hindsight, I wish I had said something to my supervisor when I felt unchallenged

---

Action Items Recap

- Start a mindfulness practice that works for you.
- Realize that setbacks are temporary, even if they don't feel so in the moment.

---

with my work. I didn't. I didn't think there was anything she would do to help. I regret I didn't say anything. (KT)

PARTING THOUGHTS

There are so many things in this world we have little control over. Libraries will close, projects will fail, administrations will change, and funding will fall through. The list goes on and on. Finding a center to weather all of those storms begins with you.

Although it is not possible to determine the outcome of every decision, personal attitude and outlook color so much. It is entirely up to you whether or not you want to make wine out of sour grapes. Be the person who sees opportunity where others see obstacles. Working to actively cultivate a positive, open attitude will serve you well beyond your professional aspirations. And the wonderful thing is you never know where that openness will take you.

Be brave. Be strong. Be positive. And soar!

REFERENCES

Azar, Beth. 2011. "Positive Psychology Advances, with Growing Pains." *Monitor on Psychology* 42 (4): 32. Accessed September 27, 2016. http://www.apa.org/.

Beard, Alison. 2014. "Mindfulness in the Age of Complexity." *Harvard Business Review*, March. Accessed August 25, 2016. https://hbr.org/.

Bergman, Manfred Max. 1998. "A Theoretical Note on the Differences between Attitudes, Opinions, and Values." *Swiss Political Science Review* 4 (2): 81–93.

Cabrera, Elizabeth F. 2012. "The Six Essentials of Workplace Positivity." *People and Strategy* 35 (1): 50–60.

Dweck, Carol S. 2007. *Mindset: The New Psychology of Success*. New York: Ballantine.

Eagly, Alice H., and Shelly Chaiken. 1998. "Attitude Structure and Function." In *The Handbook of Social Psychology*, edited by Daniel Todd Gilbert, Susan T. Fisk, and Gardner Lindzey, 269–322. New York: McGraw-Hill.

Williamson, Jeanine M., and John W. Lounsbury. 2016. "Distinctive 16 PF Personality Traits of Librarians." *Journal of Library Administration* 56 (2): 124–43.

Index

About the Author

Jamie Gray received her MLS from the University at Buffalo in 2005. Throughout her career, she has worked in a variety of settings including both academia and the clinical environment. Her interests are as varied as the library settings she has worked in, and she has been lucky enough to have her passions for teaching, experimentation, and leadership woven throughout each library experience. Early on in her career, a very wise colleague shared with Gray the idea that "it's all experimental." She has adopted that advice as a personal mantra ever since.

Over the years, Gray has had the opportunity to use her skill set on a variety of unique projects. She has worked as part of the team to develop standardized pathways of care for pediatric hospital patients; redesigned library curricular efforts around information literacy and evidence-based practice; helped to launch a reimagined freshman success program; and codeveloped an employee wellness and recognition program tailored to the particular needs of the library.

A voracious lifelong learner, Gray has participated in a number of trainings on everything from leadership, evidence-based practice, and teaching pedagogy to disaster preparedness and big data. She currently holds senior-level AHIP status through the Medical Library Association; is a trained yoga instructor; and is currently a student of the Healthcare Administration and Interprofessional Leadership MS program at the University of California–San Francisco.

$ 32.00
7/10/17